The Village

THE VILLAGE

ALICE TAYLOR

BRANDON

First published in 1992 by
Brandon Book Publishers Ltd
Dingle, Co. Kerry, Ireland

© Alice Taylor 1992

The right of Alice Taylor to be identified as author
of this work has been asserted by her in accordance
with the Copyright, Designs and Patents Act 1988.

British Library Cataloguing in Publication Data
Taylor, Alice
    Village
    I. Title
    941.7082302

ISBN 0-86322-140-8 Hardback
ISBN 0-86322-142-4 Paperback

10 9 8 7 6 5 4 3 2 1

Cover photograph of Billy in his forge in the
    summer of 1991 by Ian Bradshaw/Katz Pictures
Cover design: John Brady
Typeset by: Brandon
Printed by Richard Clay Ltd, Bungay, Suffolk

For the old people of Innishannon, from whom I learned so much; and especially for Billy of the forge, who died as the book was going to press.

Contents

Comings and Goings

THIS IS THE story of life in a village; it is the story, too, of a small shop and post office. There in the early sixties an old world was slipping out the back door while a new way of life marched in the front. Crossing the threshold of the village shop to begin my married life I witnessed the arrival of the new, and saw the last of the old world disappear.

Behind the post office a row of little houses clung together on a steep hill; in them lived old people, quite a few of whom were unmarried. Down on the main street, darned between family homes, a number of large houses were occupied by single elderly women. As one genteel old lady delicately informed me, "The best china is never taken off the shelf." Some of the old people had lived here since childhood and had worked long, hard hours during their lifetime. Most of their entertainment was homespun. They knew each other very well, as only people whose families have lived side by side for generations can know each other. Change had come in their lifetimes but, because they had lived so long with the old way, they held onto it and took it with them when they died.

Coming as a bride to their village shop I was kindly received. A farmer's wife who had herself come to the parish many years previously brought me one of her free-range chickens and a pot plant that was a cascade of pink flowers. An old man patted me on the head and said, "Good Lord! The children are getting married now!" Another viewed me appreciatively and smilingly informed me, "I'd live on one meal a day if I was married to you." But one old lady, after sizing me up from every conceivable angle, declared, "You

9

are very thin and delicate looking. I don't know will you do at all."

It was a period when career women had not yet established themselves and most women gave up their jobs to become full-time wives and mothers. Becoming one of these wives, I sailed into motherhood in the baby boom decade of the sixties when family planning had not yet become a reality. So this is also the story of an ordinary young wife and mother who was sometimes bored by the monotonous everyday routine of housework and children, and who in an effort to make life more interesting became part of the changing village scene.

Well-Heeled

NO LONG HOURS of soul-searching went into my choice of job. Career guidance was not then considered necessary and during our Leaving Certificate year my classmates and I did entrance examinations to various banks, the civil service, county councils and other venerable institutions guaranteed to keep the wolf from the door. I was called to the civil service and instructed to go to Killarney to train as a telephonist.

At that time telephones were not part of the furnishings deemed necessary in Irish farmhouses, so up until then I had only ever been within waving distance of one. The priest, the doctor, the local creamery and garda barracks were all linked into the world of telecommunications, which was controlled by Jim on an old switchboard in the local post office. I went there to view this new dimension to my life. Jim sat me down at the switchboard, which had rows of small black doors that fell forward when a subscriber rang. He put a pair of earphones on my head and plugged me into this strange little dark mahogany bench which looked like a miniature piano. It felt as if a door had been opened into my head.

I left home in October dressed up in a pair of black suede high-heeled shoes belonging to one sister, a straight black skirt belonging to another, a short white wool coat which belonged to a third and a pink jumper of my own. Having four sisters all about the same size gave each of us an extended wardrobe and it took a combined effort of sisters to render me presentable for my first job. My mother hired the local hackney-car to escort her youngest daughter on her maiden voyage into the outside world. When we arrived in Killarney she contacted a neighbour who was working in the town, and she directed us to the home of a lady in St Anne's Road for accommodation.

Behind a creaking black gate three steps led up to a concrete path which made a straight line for more steps climbing up to a white front door. On our left was a thick sheltering hedge and to our right a small green lawn. The woman who answered the sound of the black iron knocker was warm and welcoming and assured us that though she did not keep full-time guests permanently, I could stay until I got alternative accommodation. She invited my mother in for tea and as they chatted together I knew that Molly was a woman to whom my mother felt she could safely entrust her flighty daughter, confident that she would apply the brakes whenever she felt it was necessary.

On the left side of the narrow hallway a staircase led up to three bedrooms and a bathroom and two doors on the right-hand side of the hall opened into a sitting-room and kitchen. It was a warm, comfortable house and Molly whizzed around it full of good humour. It was almost as if I had never left home. We got on so well together that I stayed with her until I was transferred from Killarney.

Molly lived alone and catered for the overflow of overnight guests from a local hotel. If the guests were too many for Molly's bedroom accommodation she and I slept on foldaway beds in the sitting-room. On Saturday mornings we went down town to do the weekly shopping. The grocery shops were large and airy with fine white sawdust on some of the floors. Molly knew everybody both inside and outside the counter so they all stopped to exchange local news and I got to know the people through her. As it was winter time the tourists were gone home and it was possible to get to know the real Killarney. The people were jovial and friendly and as one man pointed out to me, "They are all the same height in Kerry."

Every Saturday evening Molly's two bachelor brothers from the home farm outside Killarney came into town to do their shopping and afterwards came up to Molly for their tea. They were smiling, rosy-faced men wearing tweed caps and belted gabardine overcoats and were full of good health and well-being. It was interesting to hear them report to Molly the week's activities on the farm. They were very shy but after the first few weeks they became accustomed to seeing me in their sister's kitchen. I looked forward to their weekly visits because as well as their friendly, wholesome presence they brought the feel of the farm into the house.

Shortly after my arrival Molly had an unexpected visit from her Uncle Mikey who had lived all his life in Australia. He was an elderly, slightly stooped figure who wore a grey hat which he never removed. He felt the cold intensely and crept around in a frozen crouch, or sat by the big black range in the kitchen which he kept packed to capacity with coal and logs. He opened all the dampers to the full so the fire roared up the chimney, turning the kitchen into a boiler-room and the rest of the house into a sub-tropical zone. Molly lived in constant fear of his burning the place down. This was a distinct possibility as Mikey was vague and absent-minded. He confused amongst other things the use of gas and electrical appliances.

Molly had a gas cooker in the corner of the kitchen and one day I came in to find that Uncle Mikey had the electric kettle plugged in and placed on top of the cooker with the gas-jet lighting under it. He was relaxing in a comfortable armchair before the red-hot range, wearing his wide-rimmed hat and puffing his big turned-down pipe. The kitchen was full of heat and steam. Uncle Mikey sat like a grey ghost shrouded in clouds of pipe smoke, totally oblivious to the conditions around him. It was difficult to know whether he would have been gassed or electrocuted, but he was certainly not going to be cold.

At that time the Killarney water supply was always giving trouble, a fact that never penetrated through to Uncle Mikey. One fine day he wrapped himself up well and went out for a short walk. When he came home he said to me, with a puzzled look on his face, "These Kerry women discuss their health problems very openly. I was coming up the street just now and one of them shouted across the road to her neighbour: 'How's your water today, Maggie?'"

Molly was a very religious person who went to 7.30 Mass in the cathedral every morning. She instructed me to go to 8 a.m. Mass in the friary, and as she would not be back in time to call me she always put the alarm clock beside my pillow before she went out. Though I protested about the early call and was reluctant to drag myself out of bed, I enjoyed the walk down Lewis Road. The early morning turf fires sent smoke curling upwards through the trees and filled the air with its peaty essence, while the mature gardens of the old houses provided interesting scenes inside each gate. The restful atmosphere and the smell of waxed wood in the friary chapel, where the long brown-robed friars glided around the altar in soundless serenity, gave a soothing start to the day.

Now for the first time in my life I had my own money in my pocket, though admittedly not very much. My pay was £4 15s and my digs cost £2 10s, so my balance of payments left me with £2 5s. I broke even most weeks and sometimes even had a slight surplus, and this I spared to buy a pair of shoes, but because they were cheap and hard they nearly crippled me. I was at the age when appearance mattered more than comfort. My biggest expense was going dancing and to the cinema. I soon discovered that although boyfriends cut down expenses they also limited freedom, whereas I enjoyed going places on my own with no strings attached. On one occasion my strings got knotted and the result caused complications.

I arrived back after the Christmas break on St Stephen's night to be met at the door by a flustered Molly. "Had you a date tonight?" she demanded.

"No," I answered in surprise.

"Well you have now then," she said emphatically. "Two of them. One is in the kitchen and the other is in the sitting-room, and neither knows that the other is here."

"Oh God!" I gasped, "how did this happen?"

"Well maybe," she admitted, "I might be responsible for Sean because I met him down town and told him you were due back tonight, though he said nothing about calling up. But I am not answerable for Pat."

"Well, we'll dispose of the one in the sitting-room first," I decided, "and when he's gone we'll send off the other." Molly agreed but before we could do anything the door-bell rang. She looked at me accusingly. "It just couldn't be," I said. But it was. When Molly came back from answering the door she said to me: "I said you weren't back, so go upstairs now and lock yourself in the bathroom and I'll tell two more lies for you." When the coast was clear I came down.

Molly decided that the only honourable course of action in the circumstances was not to go out that night, so instead of the gala time I had anticipated I had to accept early retirement. The following morning she issued a proclamation that it was to be one boyfriend or none from now on. I settled for a quiet young man who had an interesting mind and of whom she thoroughly approved. He took me to my first formal dance at which I wore a long white dress borrowed from a more sophisticated sister. Soon afterwards my escort was transferred to Dublin, so I was back to square one.

I was the junior in the office. Many of the other girls had permanent boyfriends and took me with them to dances in the towns around Killarney. Usually another girl or two kept me company in the back of the car, though sometimes I would be on my own. One night there was a quiet, red-haired lad sitting beside me. I found it impossible to make conversation with him, so after a few gallant efforts I gave up and chatted instead with the two in the front. In the dance-hall I met several people I knew from Killarney and had a very enjoyable time. After the dance I met my friends at the car and we set out for home with the red-haired silent one back in his corner. Kicking off my shoes I cuddled up in the opposite corner and dozed off. A few miles out the road I shot into wakefulness to find two arms pinned around me and beery breath wafting up my nose. A sharp slap across the face and a tug of his red hair did nothing to dispel his enthusiasm. I reached down quietly for my high-heeled, stiletto shoe and brought the steel tip down on top of his kneecap with a hard, well-aimed crack. His reflexes were perfect: he reacted instantly, folding up in his corner in agony. We travelled the rest of the journey back to Killarney, he on his side of the seat and I guarding my virtue with my high-heeled shoe on the other.

After a six-month training period on the post office switchboard I was tested by a lady known as a "travelling supervisor" whose face seemed seldom to have worn a smile. She declared me qualified and ready to take up a permanent position.

Pleased to have passed the test, I was nevertheless sorry to be leaving Killarney, where Molly's house had become a second home and the post office staff had been so good-humoured and friendly.

Working Girl

ACATTLE LORRY brought me to Bandon on a cold grey morning in March. It may not have been a very auspicious beginning to a job in a strange town, but a neighbour was bringing calves to the newly established cattle mart and gave me a lift. That morning the Bandon river was black beneath the frost-glistening bridge beside the post office. Tall houses stood shoulder to shoulder like a guard of honour over the long, narrow main street of the town.

Bandon, despite its small size, catered for so many religious denominations that one of its most outstanding features was its variety of churches, some of which presided loftily from the summits of the hills around the town. It was on the top floor of a three-storey house on the side of one of these hills that I spent my first night there. The long, narrow room under the sloping slate roof absorbed the freezing night air, and a hard bed covered with time-worn blankets offered me little protection from the cold. I spent a restless night with my knees almost frozen to my chin; by 5 a.m. I had piled the contents of my scant wardrobe on top of me, thatched with a threadbare rug which I took off the floor. First thing next morning I went out and bought two hot-water bottles.

Six girls worked in the Bandon office with a colourful supervisor in charge. She had a voice like a singing bird and though quite elderly wore enormous quantities of startlingly bright make-up and a purple knitted cap. She was a gentle lady who tried to keep us all happy. She spent most of her day sitting at a large table, counting out telephone tickets in her sing-song voice and filing them away in a small press beside her.

There were not enough trunk lines to give instant service

to the telephone subscribers at peak times, so we had to rotate calls. Sometimes a high-handed individual would demand to speak to the supervisor and insist on being put through immediately irrespective of the fact that other people had been waiting longer. The supervisor sometimes put them through if she judged it necessary. This annoyed us intensely but we could not win an argument with her; she just fluttered her eyelashes and waved her painted nails in the air like an exotic butterfly. She made grand pronouncements about priority calls and people of substance. To us they were just telephone numbers and we wanted to treat them all the same, but because she was an old native of the place, to her they were people with different needs and she treated them accordingly. She believed in personal attention.

As I was the junior in the office I was sent to post offices all over West Cork to do holiday duty, which merited very welcome extra pay. In one of these places the lady in charge made such regular pilgrimages behind the switchboard that I thought she must have part of her filing system there. There was an office cleaner in that post office who called us all "Girlie" as he was a bit confused by the ever changing number of female faces surrounding him. One night when I was working late he happened to be tidying up.

"Ever wondered, Girlie, what was in the cabinet behind the switchboard?" he asked.

"The accounts," I said in surprise.

"All kinds of accounts, Girlie," he answered, and unlocked the cabinet. He removed the stacks of telephone tickets and account books to reveal a sparkling row of small whiskey bottles behind.

In another office out-manoeuvring a randy postmaster became an exercise in agility. If he happened to be coming up the stairs after you, you needed to move fast, or else kick your heels back hard to prevent his pudgy fingers catching you by the leg. When summoned into his office your aim was never to let him come between you and the door. We constantly compared notes on his strategy. Because he was the boss he had a certain advantage, but because we were younger and fitter we could always out-run him and we took great satisfaction in hearing his laboured breathing as he panted up the stairs, knowing that he could not catch us.

After a few months in Bandon two friends and I moved into a flat together. We had enquired about finding one from many people but there had seemed to be nothing available until one evening, as we were out walking along North Main Street, we looked up at a tall house across the road and noticed that the windows on the top floor were clouded with dust and cobwebs.

"I wonder would they let that out as a flat?" I said to Nellie and Eileen.

"Let's ask," Eileen suggested. A few minutes later a surprised middle-aged lady assured us that she had never thought about the idea, but to call back the following night and she would let us know.

Two weeks later we moved in. The house was a large, rambling three-storey building where the couple lived on their own. We had two of the three rooms on the top floor, and the bathroom, with its one cold tap, was on the floor below. The rooms were big and sparsely furnished and the floorboards creaked, which made coming in late at night a bit unnerving. But the comfort of having our own fire was wonderful. The old timber fireplace had a deep grate set high off the floor and fronted by curved iron bars. It gave out great heat and the brass fender at the front had two little seats with soft leather tops at either end, and here you could sit and toast yourself on a cold evening after coming home from work. Between our kitchen and bedroom was another room which was let out a few weeks later to a young man who was teaching down the street. He had a girlfriend who lived on a farm outside the town and she brought him presents of fresh eggs and brown bread from which we benefited as well. On weekends when he and I were alone in the flat, we left both our bedroom doors open and held long-distance conversations across the rooms.

Gradually other parts of the house filled up with tenants. An old couple who had given their farm over to their son moved into one section. Every day the husband dressed up in his good suit and walked the streets of the town, but he had about him a dejected air. He sat sometimes in the garden where he looked like a trapped bird. My heart used to ache for that old man who had spent all his life with the soft fields beneath his feet and who had been accustomed to the open spaces of his farm.

One day as I came down the stairs I heard him whistling happily. I had never heard him whistling before so I stopped in surprise. "I'm going back to the old place," he said to me with a smile. Apparently the son to whom he had given the farm was building a new house, so the couple were going back to their old home. The old man looked twenty years younger and there was a new light in his eyes.

We settled happily into our flat but sometimes had to tread carefully as parts of it were suffering from age and decay. One morning as I eased open the large kitchen window, the weather-beaten frame crumbled and the entire window disappeared before my eyes to crash onto the pavement three floors below. I stretched out through the opening in the wall in amazement and peered down. Luckily nobody had been walking past at the time.

Though we were on the top floor we spent a lot of time in the kitchen on the ground floor with Dan and Mrs O'Brien. We were always welcome to call in for a chat, and they did little acts of kindness for us, such as bringing in our washing off the clothes-line in the garden. Dan was very interested in politics. At night his friends gathered into the kitchen and long political discussions were held while he sat in his high-backed chair, puffing his pipe and pronouncing upon the questions of the day. As each of us became eligible to vote he made sure that we were registered. When a general election came around he called the three of us into the kitchen on the night before polling day and with a sample voting card showed us the correct way to vote. But more important still from Dan's point of view, he instructed us to give No 1, 2 and 3 to his favourite party.

We got to know the people in the houses along the street, which included two pubs and a little shop where we bought our groceries on our way home from work. One of the publicans had a few different sources of income, including an undertaking business and a milk round. One frosty morning the milk van would not start so Billy put the milk into the hearse and gave some sleepy housewives a surprise awakening to the day. He had working for him a handyman called Jack whose job it was to dig the graves. In between jobs Jack slept in an old hay loft in the backyard. Sometimes he covered himself with hay so that Billy could not find him to give him extra work. If Jack refused to answer to prolonged calling Billy got a pike and went around poking it through the hay to root Jack out. After a few close shaves with Billy's pike Jack hit on a better plan. He crept into one of the coffins that stood waiting for a permanent tenant and slept soundly. This ruse worked on many occasions until Billy discovered his sepulchral resting place.

Some mornings we walked across town to early morning Mass. This required careful timing as one priest was always late and extremely slow while the other was a few minutes early and got through the ceremony very fast. If you arrived to find no priest on the altar it was difficult to be sure if the slow fellow had not started or the fast fellow had finished. The speedy one brought Holy Communion regularly to an old man who was confined at home. This jolly old man used to remark that, "As soon as I hear his car stop I stick out my tongue."

We joined the Legion of Mary which was involved with helping old people and we became very friendly with some of them. One lady called Miss Brown impressed us particularly.

In her eighties, she was over six feet tall and so thin and erect that her long clothes hung straight down almost as if they were still on the hanger. She favoured knitted grey cardigans over brown blouses and long black skirts, so she moved around the house like a faded ghost. On Sundays the brown blouse was replaced by a cream satin one with a cameo brooch at the neck. She was imperious and demanding and seemed to be totally alone as she never mentioned any relatives, except "my cousin the bishop" who lived in Australia.

Her overgrown garden was more than matched by her house which was crowded with dark Victorian furniture. Her front room was congested with sideboards, foggy mirrors and sagging sofas. In dull silver frames, faces yellowed with age rested on the mantelpiece, while moth-eaten red velvet curtains kept the room in a state of permanent semi-darkness. The kitchen further back along the gloomy stone corridor was from another era. Everything appeared to have lain untouched for years; the rusty range was never lit and the cooking was done on an archaic primus which sat on top of the table and coughed out black smoke when it was not handled carefully. Beneath this enormous table a smelly, long-haired old dog growled; stubbornly refusing to make friends, it responded only to Miss Brown's commands.

I moved around that kitchen in a state of perpetual nervous apprehension. Old newspapers were stacked on wobbly chairs and if I shifted anything out of my way enormous spiders were disturbed into action. One day as I moved warily around the kitchen a rat scuttled across the old range into a box of newspapers. I froze to the floor in terror, but the old dog sprang into action and cornered him in the box. When I recovered my wits I ran up the street to a friend who was also in the Legion, and while he prodded the box with a brush I stood on top of the table from where I could see but still be at a safe distance. Each time the rat poked his head out of the box the dog barked, I screamed, and Ted made another swipe with the brush. While all this pandemonium was taking place Miss Brown – who was fairly deaf – sat in her front room sewing buttons on one of her blouses. Finally Ted turned the box sideways and the rat made a dive for freedom, but the old dog – more by accident than design – turned him upside down and Ted finished him off with the brush. Every time I had to go into the kitchen after that I first peered cautiously in through a slit in the door.

Despite the fact that she had very few facilities to make her later years more comfortable, Miss Brown strove gallantly to cope and behaved always with great finesse and dignity. We dared not tidy the house as she would have resented it deeply. When she suddenly became ill we took turns at preparing her meals. The key to her front door hung on a string inside the letter-box, so we just fished it out and let ourselves in.

As my friend Sheila and I left the house late one Saturday night we arranged that I would prepare the breakfast the next day and she would take care of the lunch. The following morning when I opened the front door the old dog was whining in the hallway and there was a curious stillness in the house. I ran up the stairs two at a time and pushed open the door to Miss Brown's bedroom. She lay half in, half out of the bed. A strong smell of vomit filled the room. I eased her back into bed and cleaned things up hastily. She was breathing heavily and I knew at once that this was more than I could handle on my own. I ran to the phone across the road to call the doctor and the priest, so shocked by what I had discovered that my hand shook as I rang the numbers and my voice came out in gasps.

When I came back to the house I could hear the old woman's breathing as I climbed the stairs. I was so frightened by the sound that I stopped for a few moments outside the door summoning up the courage to go in. Crossing the room I stood at the bottom of the iron bed grasping the brass rail, just looking and listening. I had no idea what to do.

The doctor came first. He clattered up the stairs and breezed into the room. "How are you, old girl?" he asked her cheerily. But Miss Brown was in no state to respond to cheerful salutations. After a brief examination he cocked his eye at me and said: "A few hours at the most." He snapped his bag shut and left.

At that point I began to think there might yet be two corpses instead of one, but soon afterwards an overweight priest lumbered up the stairs. When he had anointed the old lady he, too, headed for the door and then, as if something about the situation had struck him as strange, he asked, "Has she any relatives?"

"No," I answered, "only a bishop in Australia."

"He's not much help now," said the priest.

"And neither are you!" I thought as he pounded down the stairs and the front door banged shut behind him. I felt like somebody on a deserted island when all the boats had pulled out.

Miss Brown and myself were on our own. The only light at the end of the tunnel was the knowledge that Sheila was due at lunchtime which was about two hours away. It was the longest two hours I ever put down. I did nothing to comfort Miss Brown. Because she had always kept everybody at a distance, it seemed like an infringement of her dignity to touch her. Not that I wanted to touch her, but I felt that I should be doing something to help, except that I did not know what. With a great sense of relief I heard the door opening and Sheila's light step on the stairs. I went out to the landing to prepare her for the situation inside.

"Oh my God! What are we supposed to do?" she asked in alarm.

"Wait until she dies, I think," I said lamely, but I felt much better with somebody to sit with me. And so we sat, one on either side of the window, looking down onto a wet, deserted Sunday-afternoon street where a cold wind whipped a newspaper back and forth. In the bed beside us the breathing became more laboured and we knelt to say the rosary and the few prayers for the dying that we knew.

We heard the front door open and a friend of Miss Brown's arrived. We were delighted to see her because she was much more competent to deal with the situation than either of us. When Miss Brown died at about four in the afternoon, the friend took charge. She dispatched Sheila to the undertaker for a habit, and told me that I would be needed to help her lay out the corpse. I was too bewildered to refuse and anyway there did not appear to be any alternative as this woman was fairly old and could not do it all by herself.

I was young and had never before seen anybody die, still less had I ever laid anyone out. My new acquaintance with death haunted me for weeks. I would wake up at night to the sound of Miss Brown's tortured breathing and the feel of her cold, clammy body. But gradually my horror faded and later I regretted that I had been of such little comfort to a dignified old lady who had died alone with nobody to hold her hand.

There were many steps on the Bandon social ladder. The old rich, the new rich, the old poor and the new poor, and on each of these steps were pockets of different religious denominations. It was like a chest of drawers, and while all drawers ran smoothly together, people were inclined to move around within their own compartment. When I asked Dan why this was so he commented tersely, "This was a garrison town; it leaves its mark." Whatever the reason, it was interesting. At first I found the town cold and austere but gradually I grew to like the old place, with its narrow winding streets on hills and the footbridge across the river. Bandon was rather like a reserved old lady, I felt, and once I began to see behind the façade I learned to appreciate its qualities.

Occasional intrusions upset this air of faded gentility. We had our own town flasher whom we christened "Johnny Walker". He crept around in a pair of knee-high wellingtons and a long black overcoat; a crumpled beret sat like an overgrown mushroom on top of his head. If you came on him unexpectedly on going around a corner, he whipped open his overcoat like double doors to display all. However, his tattered underclothes, which acted like lace curtains, rather defeated the purpose of the exercise.

At work we dealt at our switchboard with calls from smaller post offices; they passed their telephone calls on to us and we then connected them up. It all worked by numbers and nobody mentioned names, but a little old lady in one of the offices had the delightful habit of coming on when her parish priest wanted to make a call and announcing in a voice loaded with reverence: "Hold on for Fr O'Hara!" The tone of her voice suggested that we ought to genuflect in homage, and I always felt that her announcement should have been accompanied by a fanfare of trumpets.

In another office was a young man with a laughing voice who was always very pleasant, so we gave him great attention. His name was Gabriel and sometimes if I was on early morning duty I would ring him for a chat when the switchboard was quiet. Soon after my arrival in Bandon I met him when I went dancing with some of my friends to the nearby village of Innishannon.

They had there an old parish hall with a very unusual dancing arrangement. The hall was small but they had overcome this problem by extending the dance-floor outside the building. This dancing space was known as "The Platform". Early in the evening people danced outside and as it grew cooler they moved indoors, though the big old timber door was left open all night so that couples had the choice of dancing inside or out. When the main crowd was outside, any couple whose dancing gymnastics required extra space could dance in through the open doorway and have the entire hall to themselves.

As the dance-hall was on the side of the main road, passing motorists stopped and swelled the crowd as the night wore on. Many people sat on the stone wall across the road listening to the music and watching the dancers. The music was provided by records played over an amplification system. There was no entry fee but tickets were sold for a raffle if you wished to try your luck. The hall had a gay carnival atmosphere and I was delighted to have found this source of entertainment. The whole idea – a one-man show in aid of parish funds – was the brainchild of Gabriel: he provided the records, played them, made the announcements, sold the tickets – and succeeded in dancing every dance. On my first night there he swept me off my feet.

Being five foot seven I had often had to resort to flat shoes to counteract a lack of inches in my boyfriends. But after my second date with the six-foot Gabriel I bought the highest pair of high heels I could find in Bandon. It was an instinctive act of trust in our future, as I must have felt that we would at least wear out one pair of shoes together. From the day of my first dance there, Innishannon was to become a very important place in my life.

Village Roots

INNISHANNON LAY ON the banks of the river Bandon, cradled in a sheltered valley between wooded hills on the upper reaches of Kinsale harbour. Swans drifted back and forth behind the houses of the village and above them pigeons fluttered from the Gothic windows of an old church tower. This church had changed hands between different denominations down through history but now Catholic, Protestant and French Huguenots slept peacefully together around the ruins, serenaded by the dawn chorus and by the crows coming home in the evening to the wood across the river.

The Huguenots gave their name to the hill behind the forge, while midway along the main street a hill curved up to the Catholic church whose grey-white steeple looked down over the village. At the western end of the village a Church of Ireland steeple saluted the old square tower where once its faithful had prayed. On calm summer evenings the two elegant steeples and the tower lay reflected in the still waters of the river.

In medieval times an ancient ford beside the old tower had marked the first point at which animals and wagons could cross the river, so it became a major commercial route linking West Cork to the rest of the county. Innishannon developed around this ford, and grew into a large walled community surrounded by many castles. But when a bridge was built in Bandon in 1610 Innishannon was no longer vital to local commerce and soon afterwards the Bandon garrison destroyed many of its castles. Innishannon was then granted by Cromwell to an Englishman named Thomas Adderley and he built the present village in 1752. He brought in a linen industry and gave free houses to the French Huguenots; he also introduced a silk industry, for which mulberries were grown around Colony Hill where a nearby house was known as Mulberry Cottage. Adderley was a Member of Parliament for the area and was also a member of the Wide Streets Commission appointed to lay out the new street plan of Dublin. This may account for the width and character of Innishannon's main street. Adderley, however, went bankrupt and the estate passed into the hands of the Frewen family. Up to that time Innishannon House had been sited beside the river but the Frewens rebuilt it on the hill across the road from the Catholic church. This afforded them a beautiful view down over the village and the wooded river valley. Morton Frewen sat as an Irish Nationalist in Westminster and was married to Clara Jerome of New York; she was an aunt of Winston Churchill, who came to Innishannon on boyhood holidays.

Much employment was provided on the Frewen estate where local girls were trained in good housekeeping and cooking and the young men in the care of horses and gardening. Among the village people who worked in the Frewen gardens were Jerry the Pink and Tim. One day Tim decided to take things easy in a quiet corner of the garden and was stretched out enjoying a good rest when Morton Frewen came on him unexpectedly. "What are you doing, Tim?" he demanded. Because he had no alternative Tim had to admit, "Nothing, sir." Walking along, Frewen came on Jerry the Pink leaning on his spade and enjoying the view down over the river. "What are you doing, Jerry?" Frewen enquired. "I'm helping Tim," came the reply.

As well as Frewen's house there were many stately homes around Innishannon. One of them, built beside the bridge at the western end of the village, had a tennis court, while on the opposite bank of the river a Gothic castle set on the sloping hillside looked down on a croquet lawn. On summer evenings carriages swept up to the old stone bridge and while the local aristocracy played games beneath the sheltering trees on the banks of the river, village children earned six brown pennies for holding their horses.

After the 1916 Rising many of the village people who worked in these big houses were caught in the crossfire of divided loyalties. Five large Ascendancy houses, including the home of the Frewens, were burnt. When life returned to normal some of these workers found jobs in the factories and shops of Cork and Bandon, and many took the boat to England and America.

The village was a self-sufficient hive of activity. In the centre of Innishannon the focal point of activity was the mill to which the farmers came, their creaking timber carts laden with bags. In the bags were wheat, barley and oats. The wheat was milled and taken home to make the "wanway" bread that was the staple diet. Crushed oats were fed to horses and hens, and the barley to the pigs to produce sweet bacon. Two men hauled the bags up into the mill with a pulley; one was known as Jerry the Miller while the other had earned himself the title "Try-me" because whenever he was asked if he could do a job he answered simply, "Try me".

The six houses on the riverside had large gardens with steps leading down to the river; across the road the houses had long hilly gardens that climbed up to the boundary of the Frewen estate. A forge at each end of the village kept the horses shod and a harness-maker known as Happy Mickey looked after their tackling and made leather belts. Other leather work was done by the shoemaker Robin, who constantly stitched the leather *sliotars** of the children on their way home from school. Two carpentry shops made household requirements and built farmers' carts with large, spoked wheels. They also made baby baskets and coffins, so they saw things through from beginning to end. Burly was the name of the man who supplied them with nails, recognisable as his by their large flat heads.

*Hurling balls

A laundry service was maintained by an industrious woman who washed, starched and neatly ironed the village's clothes. Up the hill Robin's sister Lizzy darned and patched, while Tommy the tailor sat cross-legged at his large timber table stitching up suits for the men. He also replaced seats in trousers and turned overcoats, as garments were not thrown away until they had finally gone beyond redemption.

Innishannon's four small shops were supplied with bread by the village baker. A fowl buyer kept a shed where hens, chickens, ducks and rabbits were bought and sold. Milk was supplied by a woman whose husband kept cows in a field by the river. You brought along your gallon or jug and she filled it up using a tin pint measure. Her husband also sold potatoes and vegetables, though most of the village people tilled their own gardens. Twice a year, in spring and autumn, a fair was held when cattle from the surrounding countryside poured into the village. The country women brought in homemade butter and eggs packed with hay in timber boxes. As some women had earned the distinction of making better butter than others, it was sold in the shops under the maker's name.

Behind the four village pubs were large cobbled yards with stabling facilities for horses. The animals were tied up while their owners went shopping, drinking, to the mill or the church. Law and order was maintained by a sergeant and three guards in a barracks at the end of the village, and two schools, each adjacent to their respective churches, catered for both religious denominations.

Boats fished regularly on the river. On Sunday afternoons they became pleasure cruisers for the locals, who rowed down to Colliers' Quay, where there was a riverside pub to quench their thirst, or continued to the little quayside village of Kilmacsimon. Heavier boats were used to ferry coal up from the harbour to a large stone store beside the river. In a riverside field opposite the Church of Ireland church greyhound racing was held with a mock hare on most evenings, and the village children raced along with the dogs to bring back the hare for the next race. This field was known as the Bleach because in Adderley's time the linen had been bleached there.

Nobody followed in the footsteps of Robin the shoemaker and Happy Mickey the harness-maker when they died; the secrets of their trades went with them. Nobody took over from Tommy the tailor when he passed on, and the village lost another service. Mass-produced furniture came on the market and when Jer, one of the village carpenters, retired he was not replaced, while the owner of the other carpentry shop emigrated. Horses were being used less and less on the land so one forge became sufficient, and as methods of farming changed the mill became no longer viable.

The pubs and the shops, however, continued to prosper. The oldest shop in the village was attached to the post office and had been run by the same family for five generations. It was known simply as "Jacky's".

Jacky's

JACKY WORKED ON the assumption that most people were perfect, but his wife Peg waited for them to prove their worth. At a young age he had inherited the shop from his father, who had left many debts after him when he died. Jacky worked nights in Ford's factory in Cork and broke stones on the road with the County Council to pay off what was owed. After his sister Molly had married and moved with her husband to open a garage at the end of the village, he married Peg.

When her brother's young wife had died, Peg, because she had a great heart, cared for his children, and when she married Jacky she brought the youngest one, Gabriel, to live with them. He went to the village school and then to secondary school in Cork, cycling the fifteen miles sometimes with a book propped up on the handlebars in front of him, learning his poetry as he went along. The evenings were spent helping in the shop, where he did his lessons and learnt to speak fluent Irish, some from Irish-speaking customers but mostly from a man who came to give classes in the village hall.

Having finished school he helped Jacky and Peg to run the shop, taking over the post office accounts and the all-night telephone service. The post arrived at six in the morning and the telephone service continued around the clock, but though the hours were long Gabriel and Jacky had an amicable sharing arrangement and covered for each other. When the house next-door to the shop came up for sale they bought it and extended the business.

The long, low shop nestled between the high gables of the houses on either side. Four windows stretched across the top

33

storey and beneath them two square shop windows opened to the street, one filled with placards advertising tea and tobacco and the other incorporating a letter-box and green-edged post office notices. To the right of the windows stood bright red double doors with brass rails running across their glass panes, and a clacking brass latch which yielded only to those who understood it. The village people treated the old latch of the shop door gently, and it opened easily to their knowing touch, but it refused to co-operate with rough handling or the use of brute force. And if a persistent stranger drove open the two sides of the door there was a surprise in store, because a step down to the shop couls cause a crash landing for those not familiar with it.

The shop was dark green and had white windows and a concrete floor. Under one window a long timber stool was the seating point for discussions about Gaelic football or hurling, or for simply "passing the time of day" as Jacky was wont to describe a pleasant conversation. On a warm day he put this stool outside the door, and people sat there to wait for the bus or to have a chat.

To the right of the shop a door led into Peg's front room. On the wall beside it hung a glass-fronted press with many shelves. This was the village medicine chest. In here were cures for all ills: if you were feeling liverish then Carter's Little Liver Pills were the lads for you, and if your toes were complaining then they should wear Carnation Corn Caps. Gripe Water kept baby quiet during the day and a Steedman's Powder closed him down for the night. Black bottles of iodine could make injuries look fatal, but it did wonders for men and horses. Another dual-purpose medicine was Glauber Salts, guaranteed to keep you and your bon-hams in good running order. Evil-smelling senna pods tasted so bad that they just had to be good for you, while water-coloured peroxide made open cuts fizz like a frothy pint but could also turn you into a blonde, if that was your fancy. A wide variety of aids including cascara and Epsom salts kept the bowels of the village regular and lubricants like Sloan's Liniment oiled creaking joints into motion.

As well as keeping the body fit, this corner also catered for the mind in the form of a lending library. Or if exercise in the great outdoors was what you needed you could buy a bicycle here, too: a man's model for £4 and a lady's for £3 10s. Beside the bikes was an empty tea-chest which Jacky put outside the door every night so that the newspaper delivery man could throw the *Cork Examiner* bundles into it in the early hours of a wet morning.

Next to the medicine press was the post office, fronted by a slatted timber counter on top of which stood a black iron scales with heavy pound weights for parcels and beside it a small brass scales with tiny ounces to weigh letters. On a deep ledge halfway up the counter a row of collection boxes pleaded the causes and imparted the blessings of numerous charities. Every week Jacky put a silver half-crown into each box. Many people used this ledge as a seat while reading the paper or waiting for a phone call or for the bus. At the end of the ledge a swinging door which allowed you behind the counter always stood open, except when the village children used it for swinging back and forth. In the post office stood a small switchboard with its little black trap doors and dangling leads. Beside it a miniature window with a lace curtain looked into Peg's sitting-room from where she could keep an eye on proceedings outside.

To the left of Peg's door the stairs of the house arched across the shop and shelves were arranged under it; in the deep recesses were stacked bags of flour and sugar which had to be weighed out weekly. The sugar came in brown paper sacks and when they were empty Jacky cut them up for wrapping bread and the village children used the paper to cover their schoolbooks. Jacky had a little rostrum in one corner where he stood to do his accounts surrounded by stacks of red and black notebooks, soft covers for the weekly accounts, hard covers for the monthly, and a big brown ledger to cover longer periods. Around him timber shelves were packed with jars, tins and bottles; bananas hung off the low ceiling while boxes of tomatoes, apples and oranges sat on the red formica counter. Beneath the counter a long timber box held crusty basket, wellington and duck loaves. Beside it an old trunk provided storage space for the many differently sized paper bags for the weighing of biscuits, sweets, flour, sugar and tea. Stacked on the floor were cartons of Lux, Persil and Rinso, and timber boxes of red Lifebuoy and yellow Sunlight Soap.

Beside Jacky a door opened into the "oil house" where paraffin oil was piped in from a large drum in the backyard to fill the oil cans of the many customers who used oil heaters, cookers and primuses. On a shelf above the oil-tap was a drum of methylated spirits. Bags of chicken-mash were also stored here and on the shelves above them Jacky laid out his seed potatoes in flat boxes for early sprouting.

The shop was also the bus-stop for people coming and going from Cork and Bandon. While they waited people chatted and exchanged news, keeping an eye on the time on the post office clock which Jacky and Peg had received from the local GAA club, the Valley Rovers, when they married.

Village Wife

WHILE SWIMMING IN the impressionable and irresponsible seas of adolescence I dreamt of having seven children. The companionship of our large family had always been a source of great joy to me, so at a very young age the thought grew in the back of my mind, and there became firmly rooted, that it would be nice to have seven children. Side by side with that plan grew another, which was not to get married until the age of thirty-five. The fact that incorporating these two plans into my life would lead to hectic, action-packed middle years never dawned on me.

My heart, however, upset one plan when at the age of twenty Gabriel came along and turned on an extra light in my life. I decided that a fifteen-year wait might dim this light a little, so I did a U-turn on the thirty-five-year plan and got married, with the idea of having seven children still firmly in my head. Family planning and financial strategy never crossed my naïve mind, just rows of little girls in frilly dresses and little boys who behaved beautifully. They were going to be perfect children and I the perfect mother!

When we were children a favourite game we played in the grove behind our home was "shop", so when I married Gabriel and moved into a real village shop and post office, it was like a transition from playing games to real life. To his aunt and uncle Gabriel was perfection itself, and I soon realised that his Aunty Peg considered that she had me "on appro". That was a term used by clothes shops when they allowed you take an item home to get the family's opinion if you could not make up your mind on the spot about the purchase. One shop-owner told me that she had given a hat out one Saturday night on appro, only to see it perched on the head of a fashionable lady standing up for the gospel at Mass on Sunday and have it returned as unsuitable on the Monday morning. I don't think that Aunty Peg had such a drastic strategy in mind for me, but I soon learned that to his aunt my husband was no ordinary mortal, and no matter what high ideas I had about myself, in her opinion I needed to live up to those ideas and more.

She was a well-built, confident woman, and was known to all in the village as Aunty Peg. She had lived in the parish all her life, had the measure of most people, and never hesitated to be honest and forthright in her opinion. She loved dogs, clothes and gardening, and was a great cook. Before I got married I was living in a flat where the staple diet was beans on toast, but I often came to her for Sunday lunch and was sustained by it for a week. She enjoyed cooking, and grew most of her own vegetables. Her apple cake was a feast of juicy apples in sweet pastry. She kept her eye on me during the first few months of marriage to make sure that things were up to scratch in the culinary department, and I was very much in awe of her superior knowledge.

Peg's home was a rabbit-warren of little rooms divided by old walls three foot thick. Steep stairs twisted up into three bedrooms, but because there was no corridor we went through the first two bedrooms to get to the third. Steps led into the middle room where Jacky and Peg slept. So many holy pictures lined the walls that I sometimes thought I should whisper, it felt so like a convent. Peg, however, with her earthy language and liking for dashing hats, bore no resemblance to a reverend mother; Jacky, on the other hand, would have been quite at home in a monastery. Peg was fond of rose-patterned carpets and lace curtains with pink flowers, so the bedrooms looked like miniature gardens, except that the prevailing smell was of camphor balls.

At the foot of the stairs a stone-floored room acted as a cold room for the shop. An enormous hand-operated bacon-slicer stood in the corner and boxes of Bandon butter kept cool on the floor. In here, too, was the telephone kiosk. Behind this the bathroom was made available to distressed ladies dashing in off the bus.

Peg's main sitting-room had a roof partly made of glass which filled the room with light. In here Peg had a three-corner pine press and a large mahogany sideboard filled with ware and family mementoes. She was a great hoarder, and dusted and polished her collection of items daily.

To the front was another tiny room with no windows, where on a long leather sofa you could stretch out on a hot day and imagine that you were down a rabbit burrow, it was so cool and silent.

Next to this was the front sitting-room, the reception point for people who were to be impressed but not warmly welcomed into the bosom of the family. I always knew that the people Aunty Peg took in here were getting the grand treatment but not complete acceptance. It was her testing ground. In here was her china cabinet displaying all her best china, and the little room was packed with soft sofas and chairs and its walls covered with family photographs. Sitting in the deep recess of the window, you could watch through the lace curtains the activity on the street.

At the very back of the house, behind her main sitting-room, ran a long, narrow kitchen with low windows looking onto the garden. Outside the window Jacky's rose garden grew so close it was almost as if the garden reached into the kitchen. Peg loved flowers and filled the house with vases of them. On the morning of her wedding she had gone out into the garden of the cottage she lived in to pick her wedding bouquet, and she decorated the wedding table with wild flowers.

Gabriel and I shared a large hilly garden with Aunty Peg and Uncle Jacky and I used to love to go out there and watch Uncle Jacky at work. He gloried in his garden, making of it a wonderfully restful retreat, where hens scratched under old

apple trees and rambling roses draped over wooden arches.
He grew strawberries, blackcurrants and gooseberries and
Aunty Peg made jam in a big wide preserving pan, selling
the surplus in the shop or giving it away to her friends.
There was no obvious plan to his garden: it was full of flowers, shrubs, trees and hidden, sheltered corners. He divided
off sections with homemade fencing, some of which had
sprouted surprisingly and grown into small trees. Trailing
plants darned themselves through chicken wire and climbed
up the tree trunks. For Jacky his garden was a love affair
with nature, and he always took time to lean on his pike or
sit on a stone to have a chat. He enjoyed the shop and loved
to give some of what he had grown himself to his customers
and neighbours. Aunty Peg took great pride in the garden
and usually walked with visiting friends up the sloping pathway to cut flowers for them. The more she liked them the
bigger the bunch she gave.

As a couple they were a good combination, because while
Jacky was a sunshine person he needed the astuteness of
Aunty Peg to survive in business. He bought eggs once from
a local woman, and because he considered them too dear he
sold them at a loss. Such practices were not conducive to a
healthy balance of payments, but most of the time Aunty Peg
succeeded in balancing his innocence with realism.

In my brand-new husband I discovered that Aunty Peg had
reared a young man who was totally self-sufficient around
the house. Coming from a family where my father had never
actually poured out a cup of tea for himself this was a great
bonus. We had our own front door opening off the street into
a long narrow hallway with a straight stairs on the left. The
stairs led directly into the bathroom and to three small bedrooms over the shop. Downstairs, at the end of the hallway, a
door opened into the shop and another into the sitting-room.
A glass door led from the sitting-room into the kitchen, from
which a door led into the garden.

Gabriel was involved in every organisation in the parish,

which meant that he was out most nights. I resented this at first because he knew everybody while I knew hardly anyone, but I solved my problem by going into the shop with Jacky where I got to know all his old friends who came in late at night for a chat. There was George who was always full of fun and stories, Paddy from around the corner whose threshold of tolerance was very low, Jimmy who lived across the road, Peter who was a cattle jobber and Jim who lived in a shed. A great sense of companionship had built up between them over the years, and listening to their stories and jokes about this place so full of history gave me the feeling that I, too, could grow to love Innishannon.

Even so, when I entered this new family I walked gently for a few months in case I might do anything to disturb the peace. Despite this Aunty Peg sometimes let me know that I was far from perfect. This set me back a bit at first, until Uncle Jacky pointed out quietly that sometimes Peg had her bad days and then it was simply a case of bad luck to be in the wrong place at the wrong time. With this in mind, I learned to keep clear on such occasions. It was a system that had obviously worked well in previous years and it worked for me too. When storm clouds gathered we all kept our heads down until the sky had cleared. Then Peg was her old good-humoured self again and would bend over backwards to remedy any upset she may have caused.

As we had an all-night telephone service in the post office somebody had to be continuously on call and this often meant jumping out of bed in the middle of the night to connect calls manually. Because there were very few phones in the locality, during the day the post office became a sort of social services depot. We held the farmers' AI calls for the cattle breeding station, and the AI man collected them on his rounds. Some farmers just stood at the door of the shop and shouted in their calls: "Hereford: first time, noticed this morning." One retired British colonel who had come to Ireland to farm had his own way of delivering his summonses. In a commanding military voice he would bellow across the counter: "Send out the man with the hard hat." The first time I got this instruction I stood looking at him in wonder, but Gabriel unscrambled his code and after that I no longer needed an interpreter. An old lady with a man's black hat pulled down over her ears was far more direct. She would shout at me: "Send out the bull."

People left messages for the doctor when he was out on calls, and he would ring or come in to check if anyone was looking for him. Once when he had a home birth pending he rang just as his very pregnant patient was doing her shopping, so it was possible to assure him that all was proceeding according to plan. We held calls for Fr Mick the curate when he visited his mother. He was a very cheerful man who put his head in the door and sang out, "Alice, hold my calls"; then he would tell Gabriel, Jacky, and nearly everyone else in the village when he was going so that everybody thought it was someone else's job to know where he was. If anyone wanted to contact a person in the village or indeed within a radius of a few miles, they rang the post office, and we became the bearers of a variety of tidings, joyful and sorrowful. It was a collection point for all kinds of messages, from day-old chicks to bags of hayseed.

Sunday was the big shopping day. The countrywomen handed in their message bags and shopping lists on their way to church, and Jacky had them packed and ready for collection on their return. The old people came on Friday for their pensions. They had been reared in hard times when there was no such thing as social welfare. Always very exact about their pension books, they had them safely buried in inside pockets or deep handbags. One day, a lady whose face was a portrait of contentment and serenity remarked, "I never had so much money in my life." Another lady, who had reared a large family and worked hard all her life, burst into tears when she received a lump sum of back money due to her as a result of a delay in the processing of her pension. With tears streaming down her face she said, "What did I ever do to deserve this?" I admired the attitude to life of most of the old people, feeling sad only for the few who had grown bitter with old age.

One old lady fascinated me for a time. Once every week she came in to do her shopping. She handed her shopping bag over the counter to Jacky, and a long conversation commenced which included no mention of her messages. When he had her shopping bag full he wrote her list – which was the same each week – into her book, and she paid him for the previous week, an amount that never varied. It was a ritual the two of them habitually observed. When I asked Jacky why the little book was necessary he smiled and said, "That's the way we have always done it, and she likes it that way." His customers were always right simply because he knew them very well and understood them perfectly.

As a newcomer to the village I enjoyed getting to know the people, and the shop and post office was the ideal meeting-place because everybody came through there eventually. But it was the old people who gave me the flavour of the place. They were full of stories and unexpected comments. One gentle lady often made delicate references to the times "when the gentry were here". When I asked her one day why they had come here in the first place, she smiled sweetly before informing me acidly, "Because the pickings were good, my dear." Another old man came in every morning to read the paper but never bought it. After spending about two hours sitting on the long stool inside the window and reading every detail in absolute silence, he then threw the paper on the counter and walked out the door saying, "There isn't a bit in that bloody paper as usual." But it was George who lived next door and was blessed with a great sense of fun that I enjoyed best of all.

Job Satisfaction

GEORGE LOVED HIS work. He was the local painter and decorator, and loved the work so much that he often celebrated his enjoyment with friends. Once after having painted one of the village pubs, he ended up owing the publican more than the publican owed him for the job. Life to George was a celebration of colour, and his sign-writing was executed with skill and artistry. Long hours of painstaking precision went into his beautiful lettering. One day as he put the finishing touches to a sign his friend the local doctor came along.

"Well, George," the Doc quipped, "are you covering up your mistakes with the brush?"

"Spot on, Doc," George answered him. "I cover mine with a brush, and a shovel and spade cover yours."

George's brush may have painted colourful words, but so did his tongue, and he enjoyed a battle of caustic comments with his friend.

For a man with a quicksilver mind he looked like a blissfully disorientated, absent-minded eccentric. He did not walk but dragged his heels along in a pair of woolly bedroom slippers, wearing a long, loose cardigan almost down to his knees, while a pair of rimless spectacles hung off his nose. In conversation he smiled beguilingly at you, waving his hands in the air to illustrate a point, and swaying towards you as if imparting a blessing.

No matter to what height George's job took him he always had time to appreciate his surroundings. One day while painting the high gable end of the corner house next door, he sat on top of his ladder enjoying the view over the old tower and the river. A rusty iron brad stuck out of the wall beside him and on this George hung his gallon of paint. It was a warm sunny day with white clouds drifting across a bright blue sky. Down the street came the doctor.

"What are you doing up there, George?" he called.

George swept his brush above his head and announced dramatically: "Painting the clouds with sunshine!"

"If you fall off, I'll be painting your arse with iodine!" his friend assured him.

Later that day George was still painting happily on top of his ladder when the doctor's warning almost became a reality.

Outside the village lived a very small man known as Mór.* Late in life he had acquired a Baby Ford car, but still he maintained a donkey-and-cart approach to driving. When he drove into the village, down the hill past the church to the corner which led onto the main road, Mór ground to a halt. He then got out, walked to the front of the car, and looked up and down the street to check for oncoming traffic. Having satisfied himself that the coast was clear, he lumbered back to the car, climbed in, and drove straight across the road. Often several cars would have passed between his traffic check and his eventual foray across the road, but by some miracle he had never had an accident, though he had many close shaves and nearly caused a few heart-attacks in his time. But the fact that he was slightly deaf gave Mór a certain immunity to the abuse of angry motorists.

On that particular day Mór chugged steadily down the hill and, having checked the traffic conditions as usual, he got back into his car and started up. But by some confusion of gears the car shot into reverse and crashed into George's ladder. Luckily George had observed Mór's ground-manoeuvres from on high. He saw the old boy do a reverse barn-dance and had quickly anticipated impending disaster. Just as the Baby Ford made contact with the ladder he hastily

*Big

45

transferred himself to the iron brad where he joined the gallon of paint. Mór then danced his way forward, leaving George hanging in mid-air, and drove straight onto the main road, barely missing a Bandon creamery lorry. He drove off, completely unaware that he had left George swinging like Tarzan off the brad twenty feet above the ground.

Paddy, who lived in a little house across the road from the corner, had been sitting on his window-sill reading the evening paper, but he lowered it now to observe the more immediate action.

"What are you doing up there, George?" he enquired innocently.

"Practising for the circus," George told him, "but today's show is over! Stop acting the clown and put up that bloody ladder. Get me down out of here!"

Stubbs' List

WHEN YOU PUSHED open the protesting door of Sam's shop, an iron bell clanged to announce your arrival. Sometimes Sam came out to greet you through the cluttered opening at the back of the shop, like a wren coming out of her nest. On other occasions his head popped up between the glass jars on the counter, its movement startling you. Sam blended so completely with his surroundings that one would often be unaware of his presence.

His was the nearest thing to a draper's shop we had in the village, but he did not limit himself to drapery. All sorts of goods cascaded down the walls inside and outside the counter, leaving only a narrow pathway between the boxes for customers and a tiny space inside the counter for Sam. Sunglasses jostled for room with hot-water bottles, and Irish linen tea-towels and yellow dusters hung from hooks in front of the shelves.

In conversation he had the habit of darting his finger at your face to emphasise his point, causing you to step backwards to preserve your eyesight. One day Aunty Peg and himself began a discussion inside the door of our shop, and every time that Sam made a point with his finger Aunty Peg unconsciously took a step backwards, with the result that the conversation took them all around the shop and back again to the door.

Sam was the best-dressed man in the village. He wore a beautifully cut, hand-woven tweed suit with a matching cap, and his tie picked up one of the flecks in the tweed while his shirt gave a muted background to this exercise in colour co-ordination. The ensemble was brought to life by a bright flower in his button-hole, while peeping from beneath his well-creased pants his brown leather shoes shone in harmony with the entire colour scheme. Though he was well past his prime his skin was clear and translucent, and his tapering, delicately formed hands were without a blemish. He was small and fine-boned with deep brown eyes and as he spoke his face was a vivid picture of changing expressions. Because he was so beautifully formed, I always thought that Sam was one of those men who would have gone far in the world of ballet.

Customers kept accounts in the village shops they frequented, and most people treated this system with respect. Occasionally, though, somebody took advantage of the situation, which left the shopkeeper out of pocket. Sometimes it was because they were hard-pressed for money and in those circumstances a compromise was usually reached, but in the case of Mrs Harding there was no question of scarcity of funds, just a straightforward case of abusing the system to her advantage. She had bought a big house outside the village and went shopping in beautiful clothes and flashing jewellery. Yet after running up bills she would refuse to pay, and there did not appear to be anything that Jacky or Sam could do about it.

She travelled regularly by bus and one day as she got on it outside our door, Sam and I were chatting at the corner.

"Do you see that bitch," he said to me, "she's wearing my pink knickers and she never paid for it."

Now the normal state of pay in the world of knickers at the time was ten shillings, but this was a luxury model costing seventeen shillings and sixpence.

"Well," I said, "There's not much you can do now. You can hardly take it off her."

"It's no joke, you know," he snapped. "Bad enough if it was an ordinary pair, but to think she took me for the most expensive one in the shop! She is not finished with me yet, though," Sam assured me.

The following week as she got on the bus, Sam moved into

action. When she had taken her seat at the back of the crowded bus he followed her on board. Standing up at the front, he called out to her: "Mrs Harding, when you come home this evening, will you call in to me and pay for your knickers?"

All accounts were paid that evening. She had discovered that the village debt-collection strategy could be every bit as effective as Stubbs' List.

Angel on the Roof

WHEN I BECAME pregnant I thought that it was a miracle. Dancing with delight around the sitting-room, I almost felt that this had never before happened to anyone but me. The euphoria lasted for a few weeks, until one morning, having jumped out of bed, a wave of nausea swept over me and the bedroom turned upside down. I sat down hastily and wondered what on earth was the matter with me. The queasy feeling lasted all day and that evening when the doctor came into the shop I explained my problem. "Morning-sickness," he diagnosed happily.

"But I felt terrible all day!" I protested.

"Some people do," he assured me.

"How long will it last?"

"Oh! about six to eight weeks," he said dismissively.

"Eight weeks!"

I could not believe that this condition could continue for eight whole weeks. It was late October and the news that this misery would last until Christmas came like a terrible sentence of punishment. "Actually, the less notice you take of it the better," the doctor advised me comfortingly.

But that was easier said than done. The following Sunday morning, halfway through Mass, my stomach churned and a tidal wave of cold perspiration engulfed me. Fr Mick started to waltz around the altar and then took off in clouds of swirling mist like the Lord ascending into heaven. As he hovered in front of the stained glass windows high in the gable of the church, I clung to my seat like a swimmer trying desperately not to drown in the waves. Gradually things came back into focus. Fresh air was certainly required at that point, but as my sense of balance was temporarily impaired I stayed seated. Apart from that, to leave the church just then would have been a public announcement of a positive pregnancy test almost as effective as having it called out with the death notices. After Mass, instead of helping in the shop as I usually did, I went instead to the bathroom and studied my ashen countenance in the mirror. If pregnancy was supposed to be such a natural condition, I thought, how come I was feeling so unnatural!

I had felt the need to equip myself for the voyage into motherhood with all the knowledge that was available, so I had acquired a stack of books and magazines on pregnancy, but all the attention that morning-sickness merited was a few flippant sentences. If the misery I was now enduring was regarded as such a non-event by these experts, then how reliable were they going to prove as the further stages of pregnancy unfolded?

The tide of morning-sickness threatened to engulf me, and the only oars I found to help me ride the waves of nausea were the boxes of Rennies I chewed continually and glasses of cider vinegar, whose bitter taste gave temporary relief. I developed a total aversion to lipstick and perfume and a blinding passion for strawberries. "Morning-sickness" was a gross understatement for the day-long fog that enfolded me, but just when my feelings about pregnancy had reached their lowest point the fog lifted, and I was back once again in the normal world, able to eat, drink and enjoy life.

For the next few months good health and boundless energy were mine and I began to think of pregnancy as a golden glow of well-being. But then a ferocious pregnancy itch, aggravated during a very hot summer by the heat and the extra bulk of advanced pregnancy, almost brought me to a standstill. I decided then that spring babies were a good idea and that Mother Nature had got it right in the case of lambs and birds; I took note of it for future reference.

Waddling into the last few weeks of pregnancy I felt like a baby elephant, and one day I explained to Aunty Peg how cumbersome I felt.

"What weight are you, child?" she demanded.

"Ten and a half stone," I answered.

"What on earth are you complaining about?" she said laughing, "I'm twelve and a half stone and I'm not having anything! You'll lose that extra weight a lot easier than I'll lose mine."

Later, as I endured in hospital in Cork the agony of labour pains, I was not so sure I agreed with Aunty Peg. In the undignified position prescribed for childbirth, the pain I experienced bore little resemblance to the slight discomfort and pressure so delicately referred to in my manuals and magazines. This was sheer agonising pain, and the fact that the white-coated figures in the antiseptic production-line treated the top half of my body as purely incidental did nothing to make me feel that for them this was anything other than a mere exercise in time and motion. It was their time and I had to keep things in motion. The only thing to brighten my horizon was the sight of my ten toe-nails, which I had painted bright red before leaving home.

Because the labour was a long-drawn-out affair and I knew nothing about relaxation and breathing technique, the whole business became a nightmare from beginning to end. Chilly, wet rubber gloves investigated my lower regions and injections dulled my mind. The birth took place somewhere at the end of a long, dark tunnel and the only feeling to penetrate its density was the searing pain of the incision the gynaecologist felt was necessary to allow proceedings to continue.

When I came back to the living world again I was in my bed in the hospital ward, but still for some reason groaning with pain. An irritable nun peered down at me.

"What's the matter with you?" she demanded.

"Pain," I muttered in agony, not sure if it was real or if my mental faculties had deserted me.

"You can't be having pain," declared the nun. "Your baby is born."

I was too muddled to protest that I was not experiencing pain by some perverse choice. However, she investigated matters, then said in annoyance to a nurse she had summoned: "This one is clotting. Take her back up."

And so I was rolled back onto the trolley like a bag of flour and taken up to the chamber of horrors I had just left. This time my stomach became a piece of pastry for moulding hands to flatten out, but my mind drifted down a long, hazy corridor and escaped thankfully into the world of oblivion.

When I came back to reality I was in a quiet room looking out over a beautiful scene. Pink fingers of mid-summer dawn stretched across the city, and the glass wall of the roof-top room made me feel that I was high above the world. Mist rested along the river and the rising sun illuminated the grey and cream stone steeples that rose over the hillside houses. In a strange way I felt that I could almost fly out over this heavenly view, but then I saw that one arm was strapped to a drip and another to a blood-transfusion bottle. Beside me a very young and beautiful nun in a snow-white habit stood motionless. She looked so cold and remote that her face could have been carved in white marble, but when she turned and looked at me her expression was full of concern.

"You are all right now," she assured me gently.

"It's so peaceful up here," I said.

"Yes," she smiled. "I love this place early in the morning." As I drifted back into forgetfulness, she stood outlined against the city that rose out of the morning mists behind her, like an angel on the roof.

My newborn son was entrusted to my arms for the first time and I waited for the glow of maternal bliss that was meant to suffuse me. But nothing happened. The baby squinted up at me distrustfully, as well indeed he might, because at that stage I was far from sure of my suitability for the call of motherhood. Soon, I also began to question the suitability of one of the nuns for the vocation of maternity nursing. I christened her Sister Rasp.

The baby and I found it difficult to achieve harmony. He was not hungry when he was supposed to be hungry; he did not burp when he was supposed to burp, and he did not sleep when he was meant to either. All in all he knew nothing about routine or how to behave as a baby, but Sister Rasp was determined to mould both him and me into some kind of co-ordinated unit. Neither he nor I had a clue as to what was expected of us. I was further handicapped by a feeling of total inadequacy and fear at the awesome responsibility which, the abrasive sister assured me, was now mine.

One afternoon when my son should have been filling his stomach he decided instead that he preferred a siesta, and snuggled down for a sleep. Sister Rasp descended on us.

"Do you know something," she declared, glaring down at me. "If you don't straighten yourself out this child will die with the hunger when you go home."

But at that stage I felt that I might be dead before him. By the time each feed was over, perspiration and exhaustion were overwhelming me. I felt that having just mastered one marathon, another one was now beginning. Extensive stitching in delicate areas meant that getting in and out of bed was a feat in balancing and climbing with caution. Some of the chairs had removable bases, and this made it possible to sit down. I soon developed a sense of perfect positioning.

I shared the hospital room with a fine robust woman who made me feel distinctly inadequate. She jumped in and out of bed like a steeplechaser, and her baby was a solid ten-pounder who gulped down his feeds, belched like an old man and slept like a log. I felt that if she had given him rashers and eggs for breakfast he would have polished them off. She was designed for child-bearing and motherhood, whereas I had decided that I was designed for neither.

When the time came to go home I was delighted, feeling that I might function better on home ground with the moral support of Gabriel. But whether in hospital or at home the baby was a miniature time-bomb. He could choke, he could stifle, he could stop breathing. The potential for disaster was endless and I thought that it would be nothing short of a miracle if we both survived. On that first day at home I lurched from one crisis to another. Having got the first feed into him he promptly shot it up all over me, so we both had to change from the skin out. It was the first time I had ever changed the clothes of a tiny baby. His little bones looked like brittle twigs and I was so afraid that I would snap them that my movements were slow and hesitant. During the entire proceedings he yelled until his face was purple and waved his matchstick limbs madly. As he continued to cry I thought it best to change his napkin. That was a major operation, so I laid a book with instructive diagrams beside him on the bed. I was amazed that something which looked so simple could in fact be so complicated, but eventually the job was finished, and though the end product looked far more lumpy and untidy than its diagrammatical equivalent he was at least safely wrapped up in a napkin. But still he cried non-stop. I put him down. I picked him up. I walked around with him, but all to no avail. The wailing reached a crescendo like an orchestra in full flow. It filled the room, it filled the house and it filled my head until I thought it would explode.

Sister Rasp had been right: he was going to die. I would be the first woman ever whose baby died because his mother lacked the capabilities that every normal mother possessed. In the midst of all this self-inflicted psychoanalysis the phone rang. It was my sister.

"How are you getting on?" she enquired cheerfully.

"Dreadful!" I wailed louder than the baby. "I fed him, he vomited; I changed him and I walked around with him, and he hasn't stopped crying for two hours. I'm going to have a nervous breakdown."

"You have no time for that now," my sister informed me. "Wait until he's gone to sleep. Did you feed him again?"

"No," I answered.

"Well do," she said, "he's probably hungry."

I did as instructed and blissful, wonderful peace descended upon me, just when I was beginning to think I would never hear the sound of silence again.

During the weeks that followed the baby dominated our every waking hour. As I moved around in a constant stupor of exhaustion, behind which a backlog of old tiredness continually built up, my unobtainable dream was simply to have a full night's sleep. Often, in the small hours of the morning, as I sat on the old ottoman in the baby's room, the quietness of the dark broken only by the sound of an occasional car, I wondered if there was anyone else awake in the village besides me. I began to think that I would never again have a life of my own.

Gradually order encroached upon the chaos of first-time motherhood. Married sisters offered practical advice on the phone, the most valuable example of which was: "Put that baby into the pram and take him out the road every day for a walk. Not for his sake: for your own." Eager to find ways to cope, I did so, and on one of the first of these walks I met Lizzy May, who had assured me on my arrival in the village that I was so thin and delicate that I would not do at all.

Now she sized me up once more, and declared with the greatest satisfaction: "That baby is after making a woman out of you."

The lady in the village known simply as the Nurse lived a few doors up the street; she called regularly to help and advise but most of all to assure me that the things I was worrying about were all part of the normal pattern, and that babies were a lot tougher than they looked.

As I gradually gained in confidence I stopped my constant checking to see if my infant was still breathing and slowly it dawned on me that we were both going to survive. After about three months he was sleeping round the clock, and as I no longer suffered from exhaustion I began to enjoy him. Gabriel proved very capable and took caring for the baby in his stride. Uncle Jacky adored him; I would often go into the baby's room to find him looking down at the child in wonder. Never having had a baby in the house, he was absolutely fascinated by this new arrival, and so was I now that I had stopped worrying so much.

Soon my enthusiasm swung too far in the other direction. One day one of my sisters looked me straight in the eye and said: "He is a beautiful baby and you find him very interesting, but don't forget that to the rest of us he is not as beautiful nor as interesting – so for God's sake don't be boring me stiff with non-stop talk about him! There is nothing as dull as women who can talk about nothing but their children." Only a sister could tell me something like that and remain a friend, and from then on I tried to remember her tart advice.

When our second son was born I was surprised to find that I could now tackle with confidence an occurrence that three years earlier had disrupted my entire life. First-time motherhood is an experience that thankfully has to be endured only once in a lifetime.

Is That It?

O N A WET Monday in late summer I was sitting at the table in our small kitchen surrounded by potato peelings and dirty dishes. Gabriel had gone back to work and our eldest little boy was busy making a facepack of mashed potatoes while his baby brother banged his spoon off the tray of his high chair. The windows needed cleaning, the floor cried out for a wash and the laundry-basket upstairs overflowed with dirty clothes. The garden outside the window was obliterated by sheets of driving rain, and water ran in streams down the fogged-up glass. Hemmed in by the four walls of the kitchen, my head vibrated to the tempo of the banging spoon.

Wallowing in a sea of self-pity I thought: "Is that it?" Endless days of peeling potatoes, washing dirty clothes, and minding noisy children stretched ahead of me.

A few weeks later a "For Sale" sign appeared on the gable-end of the corner house next-door. George had come to the conclusion that he was too old for running up and down ladders and had decided to retire and live with his relatives. It was a large, rambling three-storey house with a big yard and garden at the back. "This is it," I thought. "We'll buy it and start something." What we were going to start I had no idea. One smart friend suggested a house of ill-repute, which, she assured me, would do well due to an absence of competition. Despite our lack of plans, we gathered together every penny we had and with the help of both our families we bought the corner house. Having bought it the next step was to decide what exactly we wanted to do with it, bearing in mind that we had no money for restoration. After making enquiries regarding grants we discovered that the tourist board, Bord Fáilte, was the only avenue open to us and, not quite knowing what to expect, we wrote to them and sat back to await developments.

Some weeks later, on a cold, wet, miserable winter's evening, just as I was about to bath my two grubby, tired and cranky children and put them to bed, the doorbell rang. I went to answer it, hoping that it was not somebody who had to be invited in and entertained.

Outside stood two well-groomed young men. They informed me that they were from Bord Fáilte and had come to view the premises about which I had been in correspondence with their office. Tucking one child under my arm and taking another by the hand, I led the Bord Fáilte executives around to the corner house. Any old house bereft of furniture and left empty for a period does not look its best, but as well as that I had strung a temporary clothes-line across the Dickensian kitchen and from it a line of nappies hung like grey ghosts in the shadows. As I led these impeccably-dressed men around the dusty rooms and up the creaking stairs to the dark attic, I suddenly saw it through their eyes. How shabby the whole place looked! From the expression on the face of the slightly older man I could see that he was wondering what this crazy female, already overburdened with two fretful children, intended to do with this rambling old house.

He placed his polished leather briefcase on a dusty window-sill, snapped it open and sifted through some official-looking documents.

"Well now! To bring this place up to the required standard for a registered guest-house you are talking about an invest-ment of about twenty thousand pounds," he informed me matter-of-factly.

"Twenty thousands pounds," I repeated parrot-like, trying to keep the shock out of my voice and the shattered look off my face. He might as well have said twenty million as far as I was concerned.

Then, as if to drive the final nail in the coffin where he had lain my dreams, he concluded, "You are planning this at a very difficult time, what with the present credit squeeze in the banks. They are not giving out any money right now, not even for necessities – not to mention something like this." He waved his hand dismissively at the peeling wallpaper and thumped his young, aggressive heel on a sagging floorboard. It creaked in protest. Then, having informed me that I should employ an architect on their approved list in order to qualify for a grant, the two dashing young men sat into their car and swept out of the village.

The following week the list of architects arrived by post. I got on the phone and tried to choose an understanding architect who would prove a pleasant working companion. It was almost like choosing a husband because I felt that our whole future depended on him. One came out the following day to view the premises, and he turned out to be a charming man of middle years. His attitude was so helpful and positive that I began to think that the creation of a guest-house might yet be possible. I tentatively mentioned the twenty thousand pounds estimate and he smiled sympathetically, "Ah well," he said, "we might be talking about half of that." But that was still big money, so the bank manager was about to become the next man in my life.

Up to then bank managers were to me an unknown species. I imagined them rather romantically as portly gentlemen with gold watch-chains draped across their chests, who lived behind high mahogany counters deep in the hallowed recesses of the bank where they sat in brown leather armchairs consulting weighty financial ledgers. They had had no bearing on my lifestyle because my financial resources had never necessitated the services of a financial institution. As thrift had never been my strong point, my pocket had never been more than a temporary resting place for my liquid assets. But all that was about to change.

The mahogany desk was the only thing that came up to expectations in his office: the manager looked like a footballer, and a grumpy one at that. Despite the gloomy forecasts of our two Bord Fáilte officials, I sailed into the bank full of enthusiasm, but the banker was not long in pouring cold water over me.

"Do you realise," he demanded, "that there is a severe credit squeeze on?"

"Well, we heard about it," I admitted, "but we need the money now whatever about the credit squeeze."

Because Gabriel was more of a realist than I, he had sheets of figures prepared. As the bank manager pored over them he shot another arrow.

"What makes you think that there is an opening for a large guest-house in your little village?"

I assured him that tourism was on the move, but he looked unbelievingly at me across his wide desk. I began to feel my confidence dwindling into a cold hard lump of rejection in the pit of my stomach. Bank managers, I decided, were very bad for the morale. The result of this unsatisfactory interview was that he would apply to head office for a loan, but, he assured us, he was very doubtful of our chances. He told us to ring him on a certain day when he expected that he would have the head office's decision.

Gabriel made the phone call while I stood beside him, praying. But God must have had his phone off the hook that day because our application was turned down. I stood rooted to the floor with shock and disappointment. Even though the bank manager had warned us that our chances were poor, I had still believed that the loan would come through. The alternative was unthinkable. All our hopes and the money we had scraped together were tied up in the corner house, and without development it would become a white elephant.

We went back to the bank the following day and after much negotiating came away with a loan of hundreds instead of thousands. It was far short of our requirements but enough to get moving, and we were determined to make a start. In the meantime the architect had begun to draw the plans and gradually our guest-house began to take shape. The entire plan was for seventeen bedrooms – as it had to be above a certain number to qualify for a grant – but this was to be reached in two stages. Part one reckoned on eight bedrooms opening in the first year, and the remainder would follow the year after.

When the plans had been completed we posted them off to Bord Fáilte and waited for their decision. Back came a letter stating that they did not approve and recommending certain changes. We implemented the changes and resubmitted the revised plans to Bord Fáilte. Back they came again with further recommendations, and again we did as they requested, but despite this they came back again and again and this game of volley-ball continued for weeks. Gabriel had already begun work by taking down worm-eaten partitions and was coming home late at night covered in cobwebs and dust. But we could not begin any structural changes without Bord Fáilte's approval or we could lose the grant which was vital for our financial survival. Christmas came and went but still we received no decision. Yet summer and the forthcoming tourist season were hovering on the horizon, and we just had to be ready for it.

Then another dimension to our problem came to light. A friend living in Kent pointed out that most English holidaymakers booked their holidays in January and February. As they were the backbone of the Irish tourist industry it was necessary to let them know of our existence. What were we to do? I felt in the marrow of my bones that somehow we would be ready despite all the obstacles, so I placed advertisements in the *Observer, The Lady* and some other English publications and took bookings for bedrooms that were, in my mind, fully furnished. We would have guests: now we needed a guest-house for them.

Bord Fáilte were still dragging their feet so in late January we decided the only way to get things moving was to go to Dublin, plans in hand, to get final approval.

Divine Mechanic

W E AWOKE IN the early darkness of a wild January morning to the sound of rain pounding on the roof. Our plan was to leave home before 5 a.m. and drive to Dublin. We had a 2 p.m. appointment with Bord Fáilte, and detailed plans for every minute of the rest of the day. The January sales were on in Clery's department store so we were taking advantage of the situation to buy our bed-linen, towels and blankets. We had calculated our exact curtain requirements, and felt that we might succeed in getting the material for them as well. I carried the entire colour scheme for the guest-house around in my head. We had worked out exactly what we could afford to spend on everything, and though our miniature budget was stretched to breaking point, with careful buying and a bit of luck all would be accomplished.

The deluge we met when we opened the front door was not an encouraging start to the day. The street was flooded and a harsh wind full of rain blew us back into the hallway. We collected raincoats and umbrellas and I rooted around under the stairs for an old pair of red wellingtons which I usually wore going up the garden to feed Jacky's hens. I walked through the flood in my wellingtons and threw my shoes in the back seat of the car.

As we drove out of the village water was gushing down the hills into the street; along the road to Cork it was pouring out over the ditches. The car purred on determinedly through the floods, but as we rounded a corner I held my breath: water stretched before us as far as the eye could see. It was like driving through a river, and just when we though that we were going to make it the car hiccupped and shuddered to a standstill.

We sat in the car surrounded by water. It flowed over the wheels and streamed down the windows. Up to then we had thought that all our problems were financial, but now even the weather was against us!

The possibility of not making it to Dublin could still not be considered. We had got our friend Margaret from across the road to mind the children and someone to help Jacky in the shop. It had taken a lot of phone calls and patience to get an appointment with the key people in Bord Fáilte. We just had to get there. There seemed to be no solution to our problem but divine intervention, so we sat there in the dark and said the rosary. I decided on the Glorious Mysteries beginning with the Resurrection, because we badly needed something to lift us. I know nothing about the Holy Spirit's mechanical training, but at the third Mystery the car purred into life and we were on our way.

The weather forecast on the car radio told us that road conditions all over the country were atrocious, so we decided to leave the car at Glanmire station and take the early train. It was a relief to get off the road and know that we were sure of getting to Dublin. But as I sat in the warm comfortable train looking out over water-filled fields and swollen rivers, I suddenly felt that something was not quite right. Looking down at my feet I saw to my horror that I had forgotten to change into my shoes. They were on the back seat of the car in Cork and I was on my way to Dublin in my red wellingtons.

That morning in Clery's went like a dream. We bought all our blankets, bed-linen and towels within budget. The selection of material was good value so we got curtaining for all the bedroom windows as well. The material for the lounge curtains was of a soft brown colour and cost eleven shillings per yard but before finally deciding on it we went upstairs to pick out a matching carpet. We had a long list of measurements and details in a little notebook and as I crossed them off one by one after each purchase we felt that we were making headway at last. When we had all our purchases made we decided that we had taken a big step forward.

However, when we went out to the Bord Fáilte offices in Ballsbridge we took two steps back again. We were directed to the top floor where an efficient-looking lady sat behind a large desk. As we walked across the wide expanse of carpet I found I could cost it down to the last penny after my morning in Clery's carpet department. I got an uncomfortable feeling when I noticed the lady behind the desk staring at my feet, and for the second time that day I became conscious of my red wellingtons. She was joined by two male colleagues. Together the three of them interviewed us, and again they pointed out all the problems we were facing. Finally they assured us that even if they approved our plans we would be unable to get finance for them.

We had made our journey to their office so as to get them to point out everything that was wrong with the plans, and then sit down to work on the necessary changes together and finally get the plans approved. Before leaving home it had seemed feasible that all this could be accomplished by a coming together of minds, but the longer the conversation continued the more impossible everything became. The Holy Spirit, whose job was supposed to be the enlightenment of minds, had apparently taken the day off after starting the car.

We left the Bord Fáilte office in a state of subdued shock. We were tired, cold and wet, and I felt like sitting down on the street and crying. We ran to get the bus to the station. It was packed with dripping people, some of whom looked as miserable as I felt. On the train home we were too tired to talk, and after a while Gabriel fell asleep. The day churned over in my mind. Was the whole idea crazy? The bank manager had discouraged us. Was he right? The crowd in Bord Fáilte thought we were for the birds. Were they right?

We arrived back in Cork station where a whipping cold

wind chilled us to the bone. It was difficult to imagine that only that morning we had got on the train with such high hopes. A day is a long time when the wind is blowing you backwards. Stepping between pools of water we reached our car. My shoes sat forlornly on the back seat.

We were glad to get home. We made tea and sat by the fire analysing the day's happenings. As the security and comfort of home warmed us I began to feel better, and we had a long discussion on what course of action to follow. No matter what angle we viewed our problem from, there was no ideal solution: it was a question of compromise. But we had some bookings and bed-linen and a burning urge to get started, so it seemed feasible to take a chance and start building. In any case, Bord Fáilte would not pay the grant until both parts of the plan were completed, and that was a long way down the road, so the sooner we began our journey the better.

We started rebuilding the corner house in mid-February and there followed three months of dust, mud and organised chaos. But through all the mayhem there was one bright beam and that was the determination that all the confusion was going to result in a well laid out guest-house which would be open for the early summer. It was a case of the end justifying the means and the only means available to us were hard work and long hours.

The entire building was gutted, parts of it were rebuilt, and it was completely rewired and plumbed. It had only one cold-water tap in the kitchen and an outside toilet, but we were putting wash-basins in all the bedrooms, and showers and toilets throughout. When Lizzy May had the plans explained to her she counted the number of toilets, then shook her head in wonder and remarked: "It would surely be a great place to be if you had taken a dose of salts."

The work was done by our local builder, Jerry, and his cousin Davey. Jerry was a small wiry dynamo who worked so fast that you would get a reeling in your head just watching him running up and down ladders and across wobbling scaffolding. He followed the architect's plan for the most part but when he came across something that he did not agree with he did things his own way. In the plan one long corridor was designed to have three windows. I insisted on the three but Jerry argued determinedly for only two, maintaining that three would weaken the roof. In the middle of the argument he decided that he needed more cement, and dispatched me off to Bandon for a few bags to keep him going until the lorry brought more. When I got back from Bandon the wall was built. It had just the two windows. Jerry smiled wickedly at me and said, "Alice, when you'll be building as long as I am, you'll know that I was right." And he was.

His cousin Davey was a tall, quiet young man whose tentative manner belied his prowess on the hurling and football fields, where he raced like a hare and fielded like a swallow, winning many a match for the local Valley Rovers. The two of them, who worked wordlessly and speedily, had built houses, pubs and cattle-sheds all over the parish. With them on the job was Charlie, who delivered post in the morning and always had another job lined up for the afternoon. He was a big, hefty man who could mix concrete like a cement-mixer and toss concrete blocks about as if they were tennis balls. For all his size he was a beautiful dancer, and whenever we met in the parish hall I loved to dance with him as it was like floating on air. From around the corner came Paddy, a quick-tempered, impatient little fellow. He started every morning but sometimes went home during the day if anybody said something to annoy him, though he always came back when he had cooled down. From further up the street came Mike, a light-hearted teenager who was full of the joys of life. He was witty and versatile and a great lad to have on a restoration job as he could turn his hand to anything. The plumbing was done by Kevin, an imaginative storyteller who had an assistant who sang continuously, and as Mike also had a fine voice the whole building resounded with song.

Every day I cooked lunch for the builders in our small

kitchen; they packed into it leaving a trail of yellow mud back through the hallway and sitting-room. It was pointless washing the entire area daily, so we left it till Saturday night and had a big scrub-up then. In the afternoon I brought out sandwiches and tea to the men and sometimes stretched myself to make apple-tarts; they sat around on concrete blocks and bags of cement and while they ate we discussed progress. Because the work was taking place in the centre of the village the neighbours wandered in and out, and customers visiting the shop felt free to come and offer their comments and advice. I began to put a few extra cups in the tea-basket for all the extra advisers on site.

Our two children had a great time wandering around in the sea of mud, especially the older one. The workmen had erected a pulley system to carry buckets of cement to the top floor, and he climbed up on the scaffolding and rode down in the empty bucket. The baby's chair was hooked off various support systems and though he began each day clean and pink-cheeked, by evening he was grimy, his clothes covered in a film of dust. But because he was at the centre of all the activity, he was as happy as a pig in muck.

On the site I became the clerk-of-works, ordering the building requirements and keeping supplies co-ordinated. I learned a lot about building but a lot more about builders' suppliers and every other kind of supplier as well. Nobody delivered when they said they would: the constant assurance was, "You will have it tomorrow." But it did not come tomorrow and often not for many tomorrows. I spent hours on the phone enquiring, complaining and sometimes losing my cool. I learned that if you wanted to get anything done you had to develop tunnel vision, and this I did with just one object in view: a complete guest-house ready to receive guests in the summer.

While the work progressed we went around with our heads full of costs, details of light-fittings, wash-basins and wardrobes, kitchen and dining-room requirements. My pockets were full of lists and my mind fully occupied in implementing them. Samples of carpet and other floor coverings and a collection of paint charts were laid out on the table around us as we ate, and around us in bed as we slept. While I worked on the colour plans Gabriel worked on the electrical ones. He was helping to wire the building and worked late every night while I attended to the all-night telephone service. In the early hours of the morning we fell into bed exhausted. There was no time to worry about the financial situation, which was far from healthy.

One day a salesman remarked to me as he watched the work in progress: "All this must be costing you a fortune."

"It is indeed," I answered.

"You must have a lot of money or the name of it," he said, "and one is as good as the other."

I did not enlighten him that all we had was a conviction that it would work out, and that if we could get the front door open for guests we would make enough money to pay off what we owed and reduce the bank manager to silence. As the building rose around us so did the bills, but opening-day was edging closer, too. The bank manager's voice was the background music to which the building rose, and I was grateful for the respite of Saturday and Sunday when he could not ring.

The Open Door

A T LAST THE curtains were hanging, the carpets had been laid and the dining-room was ready for action. My sisters had come to my rescue and helped by making the curtains and cleaning up after the builders. As we washed and polished, some of the neighbours dropped in to help. One lady, however, came not to help but to examine everything in great detail. She gushed effusively about how beautiful the whole place looked, but as she was going out the front door she met Mike and, raising her eyes to heaven, remarked, "Those doors upstairs look like cat's shit!" For months afterwards every time I looked at those doors her judgement of my colour sense made me smile. The doors were actually sunshine yellow and as Gabriel had wanted a darker shade her comment amused him highly.

We had been so lucky with the people who had worked with us and, in the midst of all the mud and long hours, there had been a great sense of comradeship and enjoyment. As he finished off the painting on the last day Mike laughed and said to me, "It wouldn't surprise me a bit if one day you pressed a light switch here and water came out through the bulb."

As I walked around our guest-house that night I felt a glow of satisfaction. Double glass doors led into the front hallway from where a door on the left led into the residents' lounge and one on the right opened into the dining-room. At the end of the hallway was an open office with a window into the yard and garden. Beyond it the kitchen looked out onto the street. Upstairs there were six bedrooms on the first floor and two attic bedrooms above them. Everything was in readiness for guests. We had aimed to be finished in time for the

70

tourist season and had succeeded. But the money we owed did not bear thinking about. An underlying apprehension mingled with my sense of satisfaction. Would it all work out? As I stood there wondering about the future the phone rang. It was Mrs Matchette, the wife of our local clergyman.

"I want to congratulate you and Gabriel and wish you every success," she said. "I feel that it's going to succeed beyond all your expectations."

Her phone call warmed my heart. She and her husband were two of the best-loved people in our village, and when in later years the rectory was sold and their church was serviced from the next parish our community lost a valuable dimension. Her words, coming as they did at a very opportune moment, were a great comfort and I never forgot them.

Margaret, who lived across the road, came to help me run the place while her sister took over the post office switchboard. We had to capitalize on every potential source of income and began serving meals to non-residents. It was very hard work but it had its lighter side. An old bachelor who lived alone on a hilly farm – but spent very little time there as he preferred the life of the pub – came every day for his lunch. One day when Margaret was serving him he demanded, "Did you cook this?"

"I did," she answered.

"I'm on the look-out for a wife," he told her. "Would you be interested?" At least he left her under no illusion as to his motivation.

Margaret and I got on very well together and had many moments of panic and laughter. Neither of us were very good at making brown bread so her mother came across the road every morning to turn out rows of crusty brown loaves. Margaret had previously worked in a hotel, and everything that the nuns had taught me in Drishane about household management was put into practice, too. At night we fell into bed exhausted – when we had a bed to fall into. We slept in the guest-house in case any of the residents might need something during the night, and simply took whatever room was vacant when our bedtime came. Often, however, they were all occupied, so then we slept on couches in the lounge.

Most of our guests were English, some French and German, and we had a scattering of Americans. We knew very little about catering but what we lacked in expertise we made up for in dedication and enthusiasm. We were so delighted to see our guests that we treated them all like visiting royalty. I felt so responsible for the success of their holidays that I almost felt accountable for the weather! Whatever they needed, we came up with it. We chatted with them late into the night, planned their driving routes, fixed their fishing tackle and dug for worms in the garden with them.

One morning a handsome German produced a strange-looking implement out of the boot of his car, drove it into our lawn and straight away worms shot up through the surface. I had never before seen worms evicted in this way and I protested. Even worms deserved a fair chance.

For the first time in my life I came up against the English custom of early morning tea. How anybody could wake themselves up at an ungodly hour to have a cup of tea when breakfast was not until an hour later baffled me. I was always so exhausted in the morning that I fell out of bed with my eyes shut. I discussed the practice one evening with a charming English gentleman who informed me in plummy tones: "It's one of our more civilised traits." I resisted telling him that I considered it barbaric. However, it had its lighter moments. One jolly old boy used to pretend to be asleep as you entered with the tea-tray, and then would try to whip you into bed beside him if he got half a chance. We became expert at assessing our guests and anticipating different problems. I found it especially interesting to meet the people who had booked their rooms in January and February and had given us the incentive then to keep going. They had not known, of course, that they had been booked into non-existent rooms.

THE OPEN DOOR

Many of the guests went deep-sea fishing in Kinsale and sometimes brought home some weird-looking fish. A huge, ugly cod with a large, gaping mouth stared, glassy-eyed out of the laundry basket in the corner of our kitchen for a whole evening, while the owner made regular pilgrimages to admire it and assure himself that he had really caught it. One middle-aged couple came for a night and stayed for a week. He was beautifully turned out in well-cut tweeds and had shining new fishing tackle. Every day she sat in the garden contentedly reading while he went to the river to try his luck. Finally, on the last day of his holiday, he caught a trout. He was ecstatic with delight. Now, the trout was a miniature, but to our man it was Moby Dick. That evening his patient wife bore it aloft between two disdainful fingers into the kitchen and announced: "Behold this fish, my dear, and look well at it. This sprat has cost every penny of five hundred pounds, if you add up all the equipment my husband felt was necessary for this holiday. I am holding the most expensive trout in the history of fishing." Later that evening I presented him with his five-hundred pound trout for dinner. Everybody in the dining-room gathered around the table to view his wonderful catch. He ate it with a look of such intense pleasure on his face that you could see it had made his holiday.

While some of the guests were quite content to walk through the local woods or fish in the river, many used Innishannon as a base from which to tour West Cork and Kerry. They came home in the evenings delighted with the quiet roads and people's willingness to take time to talk.

Of the eight bedrooms we had in operation the two attic ones on the top floor had low ceilings. One day as I was booking in a fast-talking little man he cocked an eye up at the ceiling and asked, "Any reduction for head-room up here, luv?" The six rooms on the first floor had double beds but when the necessity arose we converted them to twin-bedded accommodation. On many mornings we hauled beds up and down stairs and along corridors and became expert at angling them around corners. If the guests who had booked the twin-bedded room turned out to be a young couple I concluded that some of the passion had gone out of their relationship. This was not the case with one honeymoon couple whom I, with great lack of perception, booked into a room which had a new and very squeaky bed. I was earnestly requested the following morning for a silent one.

Two slightly eccentric gentlemen stayed with us for two weeks. One of them carried a black handbag over his arm which contained an amazing assortment of odds and ends he had picked up in junk shops. When the large teapot was brought into the lounge for the nightly tea he would always take it from me with a flourish and announce grandly, "Shall I be Mummy and pour, darling?" Afterwards he insisted on coming into the kitchen to wash-up. We were very sorry when the time came for them to go, because they were two lovable old boys.

We provided dinner and packed lunches as well as bed and breakfast. The day began with early-morning teas at about 7.30 and finished with late-night supper in the lounge when the guests came together to discuss their day and to compare notes. They would talk at their ease and sometimes we did not get to bed until the early hours of the morning. We did our own laundry, which made for hours of ironing, until one wonderful English lady actually took over the ironing and did it every day. She came and stayed for six weeks because she loved Innishannon, and brought with her two teenage granddaughters who became very much part of village life. They loved the village so well – and the two local boyfriends they had found – that when the time came to go home they cried all that morning. Margaret and I cried, too, as we waved them off. In the midst of all the tears Mrs Wigmore said, "Alice, my dear, you are not supposed to cry after your guests!" But she was much more than a guest. She came every summer afterwards, bringing over in different years her entire family of children and grandchildren. Her ancestors had come from one of the big houses outside the village which had changed hands years previously, so in many ways she was coming back to her roots.

That first summer proved that tourism was growing and that there was an opening in our small village for a large guest-house. Many nights we had to turn people away as we had no rooms for them. Unaware that we had gone ahead despite them, Bord Fáilte finally gave us the go-ahead to start building about a month after we had opened our doors.

The locals took a lively interest in our guest-house. One day as I was chatting with an old man at the front door, a young lady in a very brief "hot pants" passed in. His eyes followed her.

"Wouldn't she take years off you?" he said with a smile on his face.

Lizzy May, however, had a different view of the situation. "Since you opened that guest-house," she told me, "you don't know what you might see on the street!"

But our house was only one part of the changes in village life which were being brought about by many factors. Television had arrived and had immediately broadened our horizons. The emigrants of the thirties, forties and fifties were returning, bringing back different ideas and attitudes. People had begun to go abroad more on holidays, and they came home with critical comparative appraisals. All this was conducive to self-assessment, and in the process it was inevitable that other aspects of village life would change.

Men Alone

IN THE PUBS men escaped from work, the worries of life and from women. They sat around the fire on porter barrels and long timber benches, aiming an occasional long-distance spit onto the red-hot sods of turf. The smoke of Woodbine cigarettes and pipe tobacco curled upwards and blended the dim interiors together in a deepening shade of nicotine yellow.

In there land was bought and sold and matches were made. Crusty bachelors found solace in the companionship of their married brethren, with an eye perhaps to changing their single state if their friends had daughters or sisters of marriageable age. Hiring agreements with farm workers were sometimes cemented, and horses and dogs changed hands amidst great bargaining. In an effort to broaden the minds of the less well-informed, the newspaper might be read aloud by any man who considered himself the most enlightened of the gathering. But this task became more difficult as the day lengthened into night and the merriment of his companions increased. Long-forgotten poems learned in old schoolbooks were remembered and intoned aloud, and recitations such as "Dangerous Dan McGrew" and "The Green Eye of the Little Yellow God" were belted out to appreciative applause. Singers sat on the counter to hold command of their audience, and brought tears to already watering eyes with keening versions of "Mother Machree". Hob-nail boots pounded on the stone floor to a rousing rendition of "O'Donnell Abú" or "Kelly the Boy from Killane".

Travelling knights of the road related their tales of wandering to the group around the fire or sometimes played plaintive tunes on battered fiddles. Occasionally, if the night was bad and the publican in good humour, they were allowed to sleep by the fire – but their name had to be good and they had to promise to behave themselves. A good name merited drink "on the slate" but if the slate was not cleared regularly no credit was given.

In a quiet corner card games were played with deadly seriousness. The arguments which occasionally ensued were sometimes settled with a fist-fight on the stone floor, or finished on the street outside with opposing factions shouting on the participants. The pubs were officially closed after Mass on Sundays, but that posed no problem to the regular clientele, who gained access by means of a special knock which let the publican know that a good customer was thirsty.

Always in the pub was Andy, a man who lived on his wits. He celebrated with the winners and cried with the losers in every situation. Because Andy had a great thirst he had mastered the art of satisfying it by exploiting every available source of revenue. One evening I got on the bus in Cork and Batt, a well-heeled conservative teetotaller from the village, sat beside me. At the last minute a breathless Andy dashed onto the bus and gasped to Batt in desperation, "I've no money for the fare!"

Batt put his hand in his pocket, saying, "I wouldn't give you this for drink, but the bus fare is different."

As soon as Andy had the money pocketed he said, "Thanks Batt, old skin," and jumped off the bus.

Batt smiled wryly at me. "Wouldn't you think I'd have known better than to fall for that after all these years." On the journey home we chatted about Andy.

"We went to school together," Batt told me, "and Andy was always able to get out of tight corners. I remember one day the master was doling out slaps to a long row of us. Andy was next in line for the punishment when a knock came to the door. The master suspended operations to answer it. When he came back to resume hostilities Andy stood there with his palm under his oxters, jumping in agony from one leg to the other. He had a crucified expression on his face. The master assumed that he had got his portion of slaps and passed on to the next fellow." Batt smiled at the memory. I realised that he bore no malice whatever to Andy for pulling a fast one on him; it was probably just one of many over the years.

When Andy was reduced to desperation he did odd jobs and one of them was to collect messages from Jacky's for a local farmer. The list was written into a little notebook. One week the farmer added to the list: "Cash for Andy – five shillings," which Jacky handed over to him. On his way for the messages the following week Andy called into Jim for the use of a pen. This was an unusual request coming from Andy, but when enquiries accompanied the pen Jim was told it was "None of your business." When the farmer came to pay his bill at the end of the month he discovered that Andy had written "Cash for Andy" on the end of every list and Jacky had innocently paid over the money.

Andy was a schemer of considerable imagination. His sister in America had made arrangements with a Bandon publican who was also an undertaker that when her elderly father died she would cover all funeral expenses. One day Andy called to the pub with the news that the old man had passed away. They were naturally sympathetic and gave him a few consoling drinks, and he took home a supply for the wake, too. Later that evening, when he came out to make the funeral arrangements, the undertaker met Andy's father walking down the road. In an attempt to make amends for his misdeeds, Andy would sometimes offer to help out on the premises, but his good intentions did not often meet with success. One day he was helping Jeremiah to tap a keg but persisted in hitting it in the wrong place. Jeremiah got impatient and put his thumb on the exact spot. "Will you hit it right there you bloody fool!" he shouted in exasperation. Before Jeremiah had time to take away his finger, Andy made a direct hit down on top of his nail.

It was not uncommon for a publican to branch out into other kinds of business, and the publican might also be the local undertaker or hardware merchant. One pub in the village dabbled in the jewellery business, and had on hand a tray of wedding and engagement rings to oil the wheels of matrimony. An old lady once showed me her wedding and engagement rings which she had bought herself years previously. The engagement ring had cost one pound and the wedding ring ten shillings.

"Bought them myself," she assured me. "Himself would never have got round to it. And didn't they serve us as well as if they had cost a fortune?"

On the whole few women entered pubs. Only those whom maturity had clothed in an impenetrable cloak of respectability made their way into the public house. They gathered in the snug, smelling of snuff and exchanging gossip over glasses of port wine or little drops of whiskey. But they never admitted to going into the pub and their business was handled very discreetly. One Saturday evening Madge came into Jacky's after her sojourn in the snug down the road. As the shopping progressed she, in her happy state, forgot that under her shawl she had a bottle of porter for consumption at home. It slipped and crashed to the floor, where it spread out in a black cloud edged with white froth before disappearing down through the crevices between the stones. For a split second there was an embarrassed silence. Then a neighbour, who was delighted at Madge's discomfort, stooped down to pick up the cork, and handed it to Madge saying, "Here's the cork, Madge; maybe the smell will keep you going."

While most pubs had snugs where intimate groups could gather, the good publican would also open his kitchen to his better customers, who might even at times join the family for a meal. One family said the rosary every evening before the pub got busy, kneeling round the kitchen with the door open to the bar. Meanwhile, the village children gathered around the front door of the pub to listen, but they were not motivated by religious zeal. The grandfather of the house gave out the rosary in a loud, booming voice, but his prayers had turns of phrase not found in church liturgy. "Hail Mary full of grace – Sarah, there is somebody in the bar – The Lord is with thee – Tommy, will you kneel up straight? – Blessed art thou amongst woman – Will you stop whispering, Bridie – And blessed is the fruit of thy womb – How can I pray with all these distractions? – Jesus."

The village men gathered at the corner every evening, and "after the cows" they were joined by men from the farms. When the corner became too cold they returned to their pub to continue the topic under discussion. They had not far to go as each pub was within spitting distance of the corner. But with the advent of change secretive snugs were eradicated and the dark, smoky corners were cleared away. The old pubs became fresh, clean-smelling and brightly lit lounge bars with carpets on the floor. Here pipe-smoking men bathed in the natural aromas of the farmyard and exuberant young fellows looking for the *craic* had to watch their manners. They were joined by young couples and women out together who sat on soft padded stools around teak tables with beer-mats to absorb the drips. The outside toilets with the dangling iron chains were replaced by a "ladies" and "gents" off the lounge and another set off the public bar. To entertain the new customers came paid musicians, and people even dressed up now to go to the pub.

Andy, who had propped up many a pub counter in his day, protested in our shop. "My bum can't get comfortable on those bloody small soft seats. I was used to a porter keg. You can't curse and you can't spit in there now. What's left in life if you can't do that much?"

But in every changing scene there is always one who remains untouched. In our village it was Kate. She was a plump, round-faced lady, and the air and floor in Kate's had always been spotless because nobody dared to curse or spit in there. No carpet covered Kate's stone floor and no bright lights disturbed the soothing atmosphere of her small pub. People looking for a quiet drink retired there, where nobody was allowed to get too merry as their indulgence was strictly supervised. It was the teenage gathering point and their behaviour while on the premises was impeccable, because Kate ran her pub like a sacristy. After her six o'clock tea every evening she set her alarm-clock to go off at closing time. When it rang out loud and clear there was no such thing as "one for the road": her clientele filed out quietly and unquestioningly.

The decor of the village pubs had changed, but the families who owned them remained the same. They still treated the customers who frequented them with great generosity and kindness, often driving an old man home after closing time. Some of these men lived alone in poor conditions, and the pubs provided a warm resting place for them. One of the people to whom the pub provided a welcome refuge was Jim, who lived near by in a shed.

The Shed

THERE HAD BEEN three farmyards in Innishannon, and as their land lay on the outskirts of the village the cows were brought in twice daily for milking. I liked to see the cows amble through the village, but when the roads became too busy for slow-moving cows the village farmers built cow-sheds on their farms or sold their cows, and the village sheds were put to other uses. One became the home of an old man, who had worked in different jobs all his life but had no home of his own. It was a small stone building with a cobblestone floor; the roof and the door were made of galvanised iron. The only furniture was a bed and a table, and the shed had neither electricity nor water.

Despite his rough living conditions Jim was always in good humour and had perfected his own routine of survival. He got up late in the day and went to a friendly neighbour down the street where he had his dinner. She also gave him two large flasks of tea and two parcels of sandwiches. One lot was for his supper back in the shed later that night, the other for his breakfast the following morning. After his dinner, Jim went into one of the pubs, where he stayed until closing time, relishing the companionship and the pints.

The principal male meeting-point was the village corner, where the men gathered in the evenings and after Mass on Sunday. They stood in a row with their backs to the wall, holding sideways conversations with their neighbours. As nobody altered the back-to-the-wall stance for long periods, I often wondered if the entire row shared the same conversation by passing it along, or at what point it was decided to change topics. Life was observed and commented upon from the corner, where the row of philosophers provided a constant news programme for the village. Jim was always in the middle of this row, and if you wanted to know whether the bus had gone past or the time of someone's funeral, the result of a match or any other detail of local activity, then Jim could be relied upon to know.

He was a broad, low-sized man who wore a long gabardine coat that hit off his heels, and as he seldom tied his big, heavy boots he gave the impression that he was going to walk out of them. The laces trailed down the sides of the boots and the iron tips rattled off the pavement. He had a slight limp and used a walking-stick, which added to the clatter as he went along. Irrespective of the weather he always wore an open-necked shirt and a cap that was an old friend, and his grey hair curled out around it. His smiling face had a well-scrubbed look. He was pleasant and jovial and enjoyed a joke and a good yarn.

Despite the fact that Jim never complained it was the general consensus of opinion in the village that his living conditions were atrocious. When a hard, cold winter came and there was snow on the ground, it was decided that Jim should go into an old people's home in Cork where he would be warm and comfortable. Jim was delighted with the suggestion and gathered his few bits and pieces together. Fr Mick, our local curate, gave me money to buy anything that Jim might need. Amongst the items that Jim asked me to get was a new set of underwear, and I went into Bandon to buy his requirements. In the draper-shop Jimmy Desmond, who was an old friend of both Jacky's and Jim's, put all the items on the counter while we discussed how great it was that Jim was at last to get in out of the cold. Jimmy stretched a pair of long-johns out on the counter-top.

"These are very warm," he said. "Jim always wears these – likes the pure wool."

"Why is there a pocket in front?" I asked absentmindedly. Jimmy roared with laughter.

"Ask Jim when you go home," he said.

I told Jim about my offhand question as we packed his case, and he enjoyed a chuckle at my expense. When we were ready Fr Mick took him to his new home and we were all delighted for him.

The following Sunday I went to see Jim. I pushed open the heavy oak door of the home and a wave of comfortable heat and a lovely smell of wax polish enfolded me. I enquired as to Jim's whereabouts and was directed to a room on the first floor. I walked up the polished wooden staircase, looking around me with satisfaction, and thought how comfortable and warm this place was compared to the cold stone shed that Jim had left behind. The room to which I had been directed was large and airy, divided into four sections by bright floral curtains. Each corner had a bed, locker, chair, wash-basin and wardrobe. It was bright and cheery but empty, so I went along the corridor looking for Jim.

I turned the corner in the long corridor and there he stood, looking out the window. "Hello, Jim!" I called. "How are you?" He turned, and I could hardly believe what I saw. Gone was the happy, pleasant expression, and the light had died in his eyes. All his facial vitality had drained away; it was as if somebody had quenched a spark that had always glowed inside him.

He was so glad to see me and wanted to talk about nothing but the village and his friends. Even though his body was there in the old people's home, his mind and his heart were still back in the village. He never complained, never said that he was lonely, but his eyes told the whole story. He had lived all his life in and around the village; he knew everybody there and always had friends and neighbours around him to share his interests. Now he was isolated from everything that was familiar to him, and he missed his old haunts and friends.

Soon afterwards he died but something more important than Jim's body had died the day that he left the shed. At his funeral Fr Mick said to me, "Jim was like an old tree, it was too late to transplant him. We killed his roots."

God's Man in the Village

P RIESTS TO ME had always been remote figures on high altars who preached sermons with little relevance to everyday life and dispensed absolution in the musty shadows of the confessional, but Fr Mick changed all that. He was a lovable character with a good understanding of the weakness of human nature, and he would have made a wily politician.

When our parish hall began to fall down around us he decided to build a new one. The big showbands of the sixties were packing out dance-halls around the country, but in our old hall music was provided free of charge by locals playing a piano-accordion or two. Because one of them often played the organ in the church, the dancers sometimes found themselves waltzing to the strains of a hymn such as "Hail Queen of Heaven" when the relaxed musician mixed up his venues.

Parish funds were scarce, however, so Fr Mick decided to build the hall with voluntary labour, which he proceeded to organise. The secret of his success in this tactic, which he also used to clean up the local cemetery every year, was that he never stinted on praise and was always telling people just how wonderful they were. Every Sunday he stood on the altar and called out lists of names, mostly of local farmers, whose assistance he required the following week. As well as calling out their names he told them what implements to bring. He would call from the altar: "Will Bill Finn come and bring his tractor, and Batty Lynch bring a shovel and Tom Hallihan a wheelbarrow?"

So it continued every Sunday, townland by townland. It certainly brought an added dimension to church-going and some of our guests were fascinated by the extra trimmings attached to our Sunday Mass. If a helper failed to turn up his name was called out again the following Sunday, with a mild surmise as to the reason for his absence, and the hope was expressed that whatever obstacle had prevented his arrival had by now disappeared.

Jerry and Davey were put in charge of operations. Every man in the parish gave a few days work and anyone with building experience or skills in a particular trade was expected to give extra help. Fr Mick arranged meals for them in our kitchen and took them to the pub every evening for a round of drinks. Sometimes he used our phone to order goods and when deliveries were late he shouted colourful abuse over the phone at suppliers: I could sympathise with his frustration after my recent experience.

Gradually the hall took shape. Various clubs in the parish took responsibility for different sections; the dramatic society took charge of stage design and raised funds for a pair of rich red velvet curtains for the stage. Opening night was a big event. It was accompanied, naturally enough, with a good deal of the usual parochial wrangling, but all in all there was a great sense of achievement for a job well done. That night I stood at the door, filled with awe at the impressive sight that was our new hall. The wooden floor had a waxen yellow sheen, the walls glowed creamy white, contrasting with the the red curtains. The light was soft and subdued and the pleasant smell of fresh timber-work filled the air. It was a marvellous achievement for all concerned. In beside me came a local farmer, and we stood together taking it all in.

"Isn't it just beautiful?" I said, so as to give him an opportunity to voice his praise. "What do you think of it, Jack?"

He drew a deep breath before he began. "Well," he said heavily, "the hall is too small, the stage is too big and the windows are too high." And after delivering this pronouncement he drove his hands into his pockets and strode away.

"By God, Jack," I thought, "you could never be accused of swimming with the tide."

Fr Mick was delighted with the new hall, as indeed he might be, though it did have some growing pains. A very correct single lady who lived not far from the hall sought him out regularly to complain about a young couple who used her doorway for a courting session after the dances. Finally, in an effort to rekindle old memories, he asked in frustration, "Wisha, Mary, did nobody ever cuddle you up against a door?" She was not amused, and complained him to the parish priest.

He went to all the dances in the new hall and kept track of the local romances, and, indeed, was not beyond giving a reluctant swain a nudge in the right direction if things were slow in getting off the ground. Once, however, Fr Mick was faced with a situation that had progressed faster than he had anticipated – though he was not quite sure what the exact position was. Outside the village a mature couple had moved in together; nobody knew if this was just for financial reasons or otherwise. Fr Mick was equally unsure but in an effort to "tidy things up", as he called it, he visited Dick one day and as tactfully as possible enquired, "Have Kitty and yourself any notion of calling up to see me?"

"Well, do you know something, Father," Dick declared, "weren't Kitty and I talking about it in bed last night."

But though Dick's words spelled things out for Fr Mick he never succeeded in getting them "to tidy things up". Kitty maintained that Dick was so harmless in bed that it did not justify a marriage ceremony, and that she really only slept with him to keep her back warm.

The priest visited each house in the parish regularly, and so he knew everybody. One of his friends was an old man who lived out in the country and who had married late in life. For reasons best known to herself, his new and not very young wife decided that her husband was far from well, so she promptly put him to bed and kept him there. She treated him like a pet parrot, drawing trays of food to him and keeping a big fire in the bedroom for his comfort. One day when she thought that he was going to die, she summoned Fr Mick to anoint him. When he turned up the bedclothes at the end of the bed to anoint old Johnny's feet, the terrier who was asleep on the bed went for Fr Mick and would not leave his post until Johnny – who was supposed to be dying – caught him by the scruff of the neck and threw him out the window.

Also on his calling list were two old brothers who had a problem with rats in their remote farmhouse. They solved it with iron traps called "back-breakers", which snapped shut on their victims with a loud bang. One day Fr Mick sat hearing the confession of one of the old men, who was not feeling too well and lay in bed upstairs. In the middle of the confession the penitent heard a loud crash and promptly suspended operations to shout down to his brother: "Dan, we have the bastard!" before continuing his confession. Even confessions in the church could take an unusual turn. One night when he had his misdemeanours disposed of one old man announced, "Father, I have a turnip here for you," and, slipping out of his side of the confession box, he opened Fr Mick's section and landed a big purple turnip in his lap where it oozed mud onto his black soutane.

A popular song at the time recalled, "It takes so long to say goodbye, goodbye is a long long time," and I always thought it could have been written with Fr Mick in mind. When leaving after any visit it took him at least half an hour from the time he got up off the chair until he closed the door behind him. He stood up first, and then remembered something he should have told you. Then he took a few steps and thought of something else. A few more steps brought another story until finally he reached the door. There he spent five minutes talking before he opened the door, and when he had it open he stood for another session, which was unfortunate if it happened to be a cold night. All in all it took him a long time to say goodbye.

One night he sat in our kitchen as I prepared breakfast trays for the morning when an imperious guest knocked on the kitchen door and demanded, "Could I have a carafe of water in my room?"

I explained that the water from the kitchen was exactly the same as the water in his bedroom and that all the house water was perfect for drinking. He was not satisfied, however, and because the customer is always right, though some are less right than others, I assured him that I would bring his carafe of water up to him. When he had gone, Fr Mick sat there with a faraway look on his face.

"Alice, the last time I saw a craft of water," he said, "was when my mother turned a jam-pot upside down into a saucer for the chickens."

Shortly after that I saw another side to Fr Mick. One day Margaret and I went to Cork shopping for her trousseau where we had a great day and came home in high spirits. We had tea in her house across the road while her father, Jimmy, sat by the fire and chatted with us. Late that night a loud knocking came to our door. It was Margaret. She stood there, white-faced and in shock: Jimmy had just had a heart attack. We rushed across the road to find him obviously near to death. Fr Mick and the doctor came, but it was all over in a few minutes. We were all shattered by his sudden death. It was one o'clock and a long sad night stretched ahead, yet Fr Mick sat there all night, chatting and comforting the family, until it was time for him to leave to say his early morning Mass. He was a tower of strength when he was needed.

While Fr Mick would admit that some men could be a bad lot, he deemed nothing to equal the havoc that could be wrought by a completely selfish woman. Rare though they were, they could be, as he put it, "a terrification". Yet, though he understood men very well, he loved women. His only other criticism of them was that they would "marry anything". In all his years as a priest he maintained that he never ceased to be amazed at the hopeless cases that some fine women married. He said to me once, "If a woman walked up the aisle to me one day with a cock of hay, it would not surprise me."

The Second Step

THAT FIRST SUMMER in the guest-house we made enough money to pay Jerry, who had not even asked for it until the season was over. We were also able to pay the suppliers, and even the bank manager was quiet for a change. But it was only a temporary respite: the second step had yet to be taken, and that winter we went back to yellow mud and disorder.

We had survived the first season in a kitchen where the ceiling was almost touching the tops of our heads and the heat was stifling, but all that was about to change as the roof was ripped off. Of course this left us without a proper kitchen while we still had guests staying, so part of the dining-room was converted into a makeshift kitchen. The large windows of the dining-room looked onto the centre of the village. It was almost like living out on the street; all through the winter Margaret and I felt that we knew exactly where everyone in the village was at any given time. The bus-stop was just outside the window, so we became aware of the travelling habits of different people to the point where, as the months passed, we could tell who was going anywhere by bus. It was an entertaining view which made me decide that in old age I should have a window onto a village street, where instead of watching television I could watch real people.

We started our second tourist season with seventeen bedrooms. Four extra rooms were on the ground floor behind the kitchen with a side entrance catering for people to whom stairs posed a problem. Above them and the kitchen were five more bedrooms. Fitting out the additional nine bedrooms with bed-linen and towels on our budget required a repetition of the miracle of the loaves and fishes. During the

January sales my sister and I spent a tiring day in Cork
shopping for sheets and towels, until in the late afternoon I
pleaded exhaustion and the need for something to eat. I
savoured the menu and finally made my choice, glowing in
anticipation.

My sister eyed me accusingly and demanded: "Do you know
that you are going to eat the price of two towels?"

I lost my appetite there and then. We left the restaurant,
bought the two badly needed towels, and went home to have
our meal for what, she assured me, was the price of a face-
cloth.

Once again tourism boomed, with English people in particular pouring into the country. Every night we catered for
between thirty and forty people and though we worked
extremely hard we had great fun. Because we were young
and saw no problems, we sailed over many.

One very warm weekend we had a severe water shortage in
the village, and we had to appeal to guests not to have baths
for a few days. We drew buckets of water from a well at the
end of the village and filled an upstairs bath to provide a
water reserve for the toilets. At that time we had helping in
the bedrooms a teenager who was not very tuned-in to what
was going on around her. As I walked along the corridor I
heard water gurgling and ran into the bathroom to see the
last of the water disappear down the plug-hole. Betty stood
with the plug in her hand and calmly informed me, "Someone
forgot to run off their bath water." If I had been prone to
physical violence I would cheerfully have drowned her – if I
had had the water.

On another occasion it was surplus water which posed a
problem. One morning Margaret was busy at the cooker and
I was concentrating on filling dishes with marmalade and
butter when I looked down and, to my horror, water was
lapping around my feet. Where was it coming from? I
followed the stream back to its source and nearly fainted
with fright when I discovered that it was flowing from the

back corridor. The previous evening I had put an old lady into one of those downstairs bedrooms as she had a bad heart and could not climb the stairs. I ran along the corridor to her room, my heart thumping with shock, and found her sitting up in bed with a puzzled look on her face and water running down the walls around her. When I put my foot on the carpet it wobbled like jelly; water squirted up around me like a garden spray. My first thought was, "My God, she'll get a heart attack!" but in actual fact I was much nearer to having one. Because I was young and excitable I over-reacted, while she was mature and calm and took it in her stride.

"My dear," she said, "it's getting a bit damp in here."

It was a slight understatement. A pipe had burst above her ceiling and, as Mike had predicted, the water was pouring out through the bulb. There is many a true word spoken in jest but I was far from laughing that morning. The entire back corridor, all four bedrooms and a storeroom were flooded. The guests were coming down for breakfast by this time, so there was nothing to be done except act as if everything were normal – and hope to God that Gabriel, who had been summoned to the rescue, could prevent the deluge reaching the dining-room. The gallant old lady with the bad heart sailed serenely in for her breakfast, having assured me that after surviving two world wars a little Irish water-pipe was a thing of nothing.

Another flooded room was occupied by a young American who said, "Gee, honey, when I came to Ireland I didn't expect Niagara to come down my wall!" The other two rooms were occupied by two English girls who thought it all "frightfully amusing."

That day passed in a frenzy of mopping-up and carpet changing. Our plumber, Kevin, who had come to disconnect our waterfall, spent the entire day shifting beds and carpets with us. Because we had great neighbours who could always be relied on in an emergency, we were somehow back to normal that night.

Our guests loved the quiet roads and half-empty beaches of West Cork and came back in the evenings brimming with praise for the beauties of Gougane Barra, Glengarriff and Mizen Head. If they just wanted a lazy day they went to the local beach at Garretstown or rambled around nearby Kinsale with its narrow streets and historic forts, while those who wanted to do nothing simply sat by the river or went to the wood for the day. At night they visited the pubs where they met the locals; the favourite pub was Kate's where they, too, obeyed the ring of the alarm clock.

Andy was delighted with the tourists and was always strategically placed if bags had to be carried in from cars. One evening towards the end of summer a girl arrived on the bus laden with a case full of books – she was coming to teach in the local school. Andy dashed to her rescue and swept the case from her, drowning her protestations about being able to carry it herself. Later, in the dining-room she remarked on his gallantry. In the months that followed when she came to know him better, and had paid well for his consideration, she often laughed about that first evening. But she always insisted that he had made a great impression on her arrival.

Little Bits of Paper

THE LATE SIXTIES and early seventies were boom years for Irish tourism. The English holiday-makers turned their faces towards Ireland, and every morning when the Cork-Swansea ferry berthed streams of GB cars drove into West Cork. People from the North of Ireland came south, and the summer that the first of the Northern troubles started our guest-house was full of Northern Unionists, many of whom had come on the recommendation of friends who had stayed previously.

Some English families came back year after year. The English made wonderful guests: they were punctual, considerate and appreciative. But some held very strange ideas about Ireland. One elderly couple who came to us via Rosslare were amazed at the distance they had had to travel. The husband said, "I thought that we could walk from Rosslare to your guest-house. I actually though that we could drive around the whole of Ireland in an hour." Another dapper little man with a BBC accent kept referring to "the mainland" in conversation. It took me a while to figure out that to him England was the mainland, and that we were just an off-shore island.

As the Northern troubles gathered momentum the flow of English tourists trickled to a halt, and a door closed firmly between North and South. By then our family of two sons had increased to four and Uncle Jacky had suffered a slight heart-attack. Between the guest-house, the post office and the shop we were over-stretched; our workload would have to be reduced somehow, and Jacky needed more help in the shop. As the shop had been in the family for five generations it took precedence over the guest-house, which did not have the same historical roots. We decided to convert part of the guest-house into flats and so reduce the amount of time and work it demanded.

That winter I went back to help in the shop, and the first thing Jacky said to me was, "Alice, will you sort out the accounts for the blessed tax crowd?" A few years previously turnover tax – the forerunner of VAT – had reared its ugly head and Jacky, like a lot of older shopkeepers in rural Ireland, had no idea how to handle it. Though quite willing to pay, they had no accounting system to assess what they owed. Jacky handed over boxes and boxes of invoices with a sigh of relief. "Thanks be to God to be rid of these, they have the life worried out of me," he said.

So began days of sorting cardboard boxes, and trying to bring some kind of order to years of invoices. As days turned into weeks the boxes emptied, while all around our sitting-room floor and over the furniture mountains of invoices rose, sorted under the names of different firms. Our children trod carefully between the paper mountains, and kept me at a safe distance. Their normally tranquil mother was fast turning into a paper-sorting maniac who talked aloud to herself and used language "that the strangers do not know".

When all was sorted we bought a large filing cabinet and gradually our sitting-room reappeared as hills do when a thaw comes after snow. But then the real work began, as I tried to pull together some shape or form of accounts. This went on for weeks until my nerves started to fray from the continual concentration. Jacky would come to the door with a worried look on his face and ask with concern, "How are you getting on?" And because I would not upset him for the world, I would say, "Grand altogether, it will all work out fine."

But I had my doubts and finally one evening when weeks of work and sheets of figures would not balance, I threw the cash-book on the floor and stormed out to the guest-house kitchen. There my mother who was on one of her regular visits stood in front of the Aga, serenely stirring rice for the children. "Would you like a cup of tea?" she asked.

"Mom!" I shouted, pounding the table with my fist, "The accounts are driving me crazy! They just will not balance out."

She said nothing for a few minutes and let me rant on. When I had finished she smiled and said, "Sit down there now and have a cup of tea and I'll make toast for you." She always had great faith in the comforting power of warm toast. As we sat having our tea and toast she said quietly, "Alice, I never thought I'd see the day that you'd get so upset about little bits of paper. Don't ever forget that's all they are – little bits of paper." I started to laugh, and in the face of her simple logic the problem came into perspective.

Eventually I brought the shop accounts up to date, and Jacky was so relieved that it made all the effort worthwhile.

It was Aunty Peg as usual who had the last word. "I'll tell you something," she said, shaking her finger at me. "You're learning to do too much. It's a big mistake! The more you can do the more you will have to do."

But I was glad to be back in the shop with Jacky, who was so very much in touch with the people and everything that went on in the village, including one of the great loves of his life, the GAA.

"Come on the Rovers"

THERE WERE TWO religious denominations in the village, Church of Ireland and Roman Catholic, and while they prayed in separate churches they came together on every other occasion. When the local GAA team, the Valley Rovers, was playing they prayed together on the sideline for victory, and the ecumenical hymn that sometimes rose to fever pitch was "Come on the Rovers."

There was one pair of vocal cords that rose above all others and pierced the air with the velocity of a zooming *sliotar*: Joe's "Come on the Rovers" was sometimes more effective in winning matches than all the pep-talks and pre-match instructions put together. He had another refrain which was heard at every match. As soon as a ball headed for the sideline he would forecast "Tha-a-at's a Roov-ers' baawl!" Though it was advisable, out of respect for your eardrums, not to stand too close to him, Joe brought an inimitable flavour to the matches.

Every Sunday after Mass a crowd gathered at the corner and the available cars were packed to capacity to carry people to the matches. There was no question of leaving anybody behind, even if they had to be crammed into the boot. On Monday morning the replay started early in our shop with the arrival of the postmen to sort the mail. It continued all day. The match under discussion could be a Rovers or a Bandon game, or indeed any game that had been played the day before. Frees were retaken, referees' decisions questioned and every kick of the game analysed. Commercial travellers and delivery men joined the post mortems and GAA stalwarts called in to air their views. Late that night when Jacky's old buddies came in, the final count was held.

97

Then, after closing the shop, Jacky took all the daily papers and read every match report; afterwards he and Gabriel analysed the reporters' analyses of the game. Next to God the GAA was the most important thing in the house, or indeed the village. Jacky had played, refereed and been on the local and divisional boards at different stages of his life, and Gabriel followed in his footsteps.

I had never even been at a GAA match before getting married, so I was mesmerised by all this dedication which hit me with the ferocity of a gale-force wind. To maintain a sane balance in the house, I decided that I should keep my distance from the athletic activities. But Aunty Peg rocked my detachment when she threw a box of Rovers jerseys into the kitchen saying, "I've been minding these long enough; it's about time someone else took over." So on many Mondays when I wanted to hang out my washing, it had to take second place to rows of Rovers jerseys fluttering in the breeze. Gradually, however, I became drawn into this sea of enthusiasm and was caught up in the match fever. The people who attended the games were equally fascinating. It was amazing to watch dour men, men who would normally hardly pass the time of day with you, explode in a frenzy of exultation that caused them to shoot into the air like rockets whenever their side scored. Bring together hundreds of such men and you have the dynamic atmosphere of a Munster or All-Ireland Final.

On my first visit to Dublin's GAA Mecca, Croke Park, we went into the restaurant under the stands, and while Gabriel queued for tea and cakes I became absorbed in watching the people around me. I saw the well-fed city business man, his overflowing paunch controlled by a well-cut suit, out for the day with "the boys". The hardy, weather-beaten country bachelor in his ten-year-old suit had made the journey on his own, and carried his sandwiches wrapped in brown paper under his arm. Used to solitary living, he needed no one to share his day. There was the professional from the country accompanied by his expensively-dressed, sun-tanned wife wearing good shoes and pricey jewellery; in tow a bored teenager. Then came a little woman with a plastic bag full of sandwiches, followed by a row of children, "himself" bringing up the rear in a brown suit and hand-knitted pullover. She fussed around making sure that they were all well fed, while the eldest ferried cups of tea to the family and himself pulled on a cigarette, his mind occupied with greater things. A thin, self-sufficient Christian Brother catered for himself in another corner; his black beret poked out of his pocket and a plastic mac lay folded neatly beside him.

A group of tanned young country fellows broke on the scene, laughing and shouting together, trying to outdo one another in acting the "hard man". Next to them stood two gorgeous girls in floral sun-dresses with long blonde hair. An overweight priest pontificated in a loud voice as if he were still giving the morning sermon, while a hard-faced, strident woman belted talk into the face of a resigned husband, who looked around hoping to see someone he might know. Out for the day a father and son, not sure if they were boys together or men.

Behind me two countrymen discussed the match. "Our fellows are bigger and stronger; that should count for some-thing," one man asserted confidently.

"That's not the way it goes," his friend cautioned. "The other lads are small and handy and could be hard to handle. If we are to win today, our fellows might have to lower the blade a bit!"

The Artane Boys Band thundered by on their way to the playing pitch, and we all filed out and up the steps into the blazing excitement of the All-Ireland Final.

When Fr Mick had been transferred to another parish he was replaced by Fr Seamus, a keen sports enthusiast. He trained the schoolchildren and the under-age GAA shot into prominence; we fielded under-12s, -14s, and -16s and they went on to win not only divisional but county championships.

Women like myself, who up until then hardly knew the difference between a *sliotar* and a football, became sideline experts overnight. One evening Gabriel was refereeing a Rovers game, and he was bending over backwards not to show favouritism to the local side. When he overlooked a bit of rough play by the opposing team, totally taken up with the game I shouted, "Hi! Ref, did you see that?" Coming off the field afterwards, Fr Seamus and himself were discussing the game. "Everyone seemed to be happy enough with the way things went," Gabriel said. "There was only one objection during the whole match."

"That," Fr Seamus informed him, "was from your own wife."

The Rovers practised in many fields around the parish until they bought their own pitch. Beautifully situated at the western end of the village by the river, it was never called the football field, but was known simply as "the Bleach". It was here that Adderley had had his linen bleached in former times. It had a slight problem in that the river, which was tidal, caused occasional flooding, but in time that was overcome. Later a stately row of elms inside the Bleach wall near the pitch was considered dangerous to passing traffic, and a felling order was sought. Feelings about the trees ran high in the village so a meeting was called, but in the end it was agreed that the trees had to go. The day that the trees came down our village lost some if its grandeur: they had towered over the western end for almost a hundred years.

The Valley Rovers hurling and football teams brought much enjoyment to the people of the parish; there was no mistaking how much it meant on the day that they won the County Final for the first time. As I walked through the village that night the faces along the street were alive with delight. Old Rovers in the winter of their years were laughing and dancing around like boys. Playing the game had been one of the highlights of their young lives and now in old age this club victory was giving them a new sense of excitement. Women who had cheered on brothers, boyfriends and sons from the sideline were out to celebrate with their menfolk in the pubs and the parish hall. It was a great night for the Valley Rovers and the parish.

The parish hall and the Bleach provided excellent facilities for the people of the parish. A generous parishioner donated a tennis court and later the Rovers built dressing rooms behind the hall. When the little Church of Ireland school across the road ceased to function because the students were transferred to nearby Bandon, the building, known as the Bridge hall, became available for table-tennis, music and art classes.

Paddy was the man who kept his eye on all parish property. He was caretaker of the parish hall but his duties did not end there. He kept track of everything around the village, collecting newspapers off the bus, digging gardens for the old ladies – even forecasting the weather. He kept a large tory-top on his window-sill: the pinecone opened wide if the weather was going to be fine and closed up in preparation for rain. It was seldom wrong.

When Gabriel was refereeing Paddy always acted as one of the linesmen, and no one questioned Paddy's decisions because he had the temperament of a wasp. Yet he had a wonderful way with children – the baby in our family travelled to the matches on his knee. The village children visited Paddy regularly, and he told them far-fetched stories about "Herself Upstairs." Though they never saw her they believed that he had a wife upstairs because he told them such great stories about her. They behaved beautifully while they were in the house because Paddy had them warned that "Herself was a holy terror" and that if they misbehaved she would come down and wallop them.

His small stone house, which he painted every year with yellow ochre, was right across the road from our back gate, so Paddy supervised all our comings and goings. When we had a rather strange lady come to stay, he had a busy time keeping track of her.

The Case under the Bed

IT WAS A MORNING in late September and I was sitting in an armchair in the kitchen with my feet up, reading the paper. Breakfast was over, the dining-room had been cleared and the guest-rooms tidied and I was enjoying the leisure and relaxation of the moment when the service bell buzzed in the kitchen. I reluctantly dragged myself out of the armchair and as I walked along the corridor made a mental check of the accommodation available. The five bedrooms were full and I had only one holiday flat free, but as we were closing down for the season at the end of the month it was only available for a week.

When I rounded the corner leading into the front hallway I saw a petite figure with bobbed silver-blonde or grey hair standing before me. With the light from the glass door behind her I could not be certain of her hair colour, or indeed of her age. She could have been anything between twenty-five and fifty-five; her face was childlike and ageless, and she had about her a waif-like appearance. She wore a bright red jacket over a long black skirt and had the figure of a slim teenager.

"Have you got a furnished flat to let?" she asked in a precise upper-class English accent.

She did not address her question directly to me but to some vague point in the air above my head. Her eyes were a deep golden brown but they did not seem to focus; they drifted away to a distant place where her mind had wandered. There was something almost unreal about this woman: though her body was before me her mind and concentration had floated away somewhere else.

"Well, we have one holiday flat but it's only available for

one week as we will be closing for the season," I told her.

"May I see it?" she lisped in a childish voice.

I led her upstairs and as she inspected the rooms her face remained expressionless.

"For how long do you need a flat?" I asked in an effort to get some facts established.

"Difficult to know," she answered vaguely.

"Well," I repeated, "this is only available for one week. Do you need long-term accommodation?"

"I think I do," she answered in a surprised voice, as if she had just discovered the fact.

"Well then," I said firmly, "that settles it, because these are only holiday flats and we will be closing them down for the winter next week."

"Why?"

"Because ..." I started, but she was not really listening.

"Do you own this place?" she asked. I told her that I did and introduced myself and asked for similar details.

"I am Penelope Ann Carter Page," she informed me grandly.

As we returned to the front door she waltzed along ahead of me humming to herself. "Day-day," she waved, smiling vaguely, and went out the door fluttering her fingers in the air like a baby practising its first goodbye. I went back to the kitchen and put the kettle on the Aga to make a cup of tea before going into Cork to do some shopping.

When I came home that evening my seven-year-old met me in the front hallway, jumping with delight and bubbling over with his exciting news. "Mammy," he shouted, "a lady booked in with a wheelbarrow."

"With a what?" I demanded.

"A wheelbarrow, a wheelbarrow," he chanted, running around the hall pushing an imaginary wheelbarrow in front of him to demonstrate the reality of the situation.

"But what was in it?" I asked apprehensively.

"A dog!" he announced with delight.

"A dog?"

"Sitting inside in the wheelbarrow between clothes and books and – and a saucepan," he finished triumphantly.

"Oh my God!" I gasped, raising my eyes to heaven. "Where is she now?"

"Upstairs in the end flat."

"But who booked her in?" I demanded.

"No one," he said, surprised that I should be asking such a stupid question. "She knew where it was, and I took her books up for her."

"But this is impossible," I protested, feeling that I was at the Mad Hatter's tea-party. "She can't move in just like that!"

"But she is in," he declared, "and she's a nice lady and she likes it and I like her."

Enquiries to other members of the household bore out the truth of his story. On hearing of our unusual guest and her strange arrival the two older children thought that it was very funny, as indeed did some of the neighbours. If Lizzy May had been one of them, I thought, she would have concluded that I had opened a home for waifs and strays.

Apparently Penelope Ann had stayed for a few days in a hotel outside the village and had borrowed their wheelbarrow to transport her belongings to her new-found accommodation. When she had herself installed, she pushed the barrow back down to the hotel with the dog sitting inside like a queen in a royal coach. She had not yet returned.

Later, with the dog on a long lead, she swept in the front door and up the stairs as if she had been in the house all her life. I decided that I had better try to get things sorted out so I followed her up. But it was impossible to sort out Penelope Ann: she did not listen; she just gazed over my head. I could not get through to her because she shut a mental door against me.

I rang the hotel to try to get some background to the situation. The manager told me that she had arrived a few days previously and had an English address, but he thought she had been in Ireland for a long time. "Actually," he said, "she's OK. It's the dog that's the problem."

How right he was! That dog became the bane of my life. His name was Junky and he was well christened, because if junk food is the lowest form of sustenance Junky, too, was well down the canine ladder of quality. Somewhere in his mixed genealogy a greyhound and a terrier had had a few moments of togetherness and Junky had inherited their worst traits; a sheepdog had also crossed his ancestral path somewhere back along the line. But if I thought that Junky was the lowest form of dog life, for Penelope Ann he was the reason for living.

Junky had our backyard and garden to himself and night after night he pulled and played with everything that hung off the clothes-line. I collected torn sheets and towels from the four corners of the garden and prayed for patience. Penelope Ann refused all requests to tie him up at night and if I did so she promptly came down and released him. Nevertheless she lived in constant fear that he might escape from the backyard and run away, so in case anybody might open the back gate she collected dozens of crates from behind the shop and stacked them up inside the gate. When Paddy, upstairs in his house across the road, saw her do this he put his head out the window and shouted at her to stop, but she was deaf to everything but the needs of Junky. Trying to put a car into the yard we pushed vainly against the gate from outside but it stood unyielding, held firmly in position by stacks of crates. So then we had to come in through the house and shift all the crates. This drove everybody crazy when we had to do it time after time but, when we asked Penelope Ann to stop barricading our backyard, she just smiled and continued merrily on her way.

Despite all her precautions I awoke early one morning to calls of "Junky! Junky! Junky!" coming from the street. Penelope Ann stood on the white line in the middle of the road with traffic whizzing past her; annoyed motorists shook their fists and blew their horns, but she was oblivious to everything but the missing dog. Her cry of "Junky, Junky" rose to a piercing wail. A neighbour up the street called Julia thought that she was being called and came to her front door, and gradually most of the village emerged to witness the scene. I tried to talk her off the road but she ignored me, until finally Junky appeared. He looked quite pleased with himself after his escapade and was welcomed back like the prodigal son, though gently reprimanded and told to be a "better boy".

One day soon after this episode I met Lizzy May, who had evidently decided that I needed some counselling. "Do you realise, my dear," she said, "that little lady with the strange dog is not playing with the full deck." As Lizzy May was a serious card-player I got her meaning straight away, but I did not tell her that if the same little lady stayed much longer, I'd be minus a few cards myself.

During the months that Penelope Ann was with us a "boy" was what I presumed Junky to be, because she always addressed him as such. But life around Penelope Ann was full of the unexpected. After the escape she kept Junky in her flat and absolutely refused to let him out in the backyard again. Occasionally they passed me in the corridor as she led him out for his regular walk. On one of these occasions I was delicately balanced on top of a chair reaching up to paint the ceiling with a big tin of white paint beside me, which Junky on his rush past promptly turned upside down. As I glared after him I noticed that he had grown decidedly plump and thought that Penelope Ann must be feeding him too well. A few days later I met Junky on the stairs again; he was drastically reduced in size. Hardly able to believe my eyes, I realised that he had a pronounced post-natal appearance. Was it possible? I stood halfway up the stairs, shocked to a standstill. As my mind grappled to change its concept of Junky's sex, I realised too that if there were pups, they had to be hidden somewhere.

I waited until she came back from her walk.

"Where are they?" I demanded.

"Come along and meet them," she invited with a beaming smile, delighted to share the joy of motherhood with me. She waltzed into the bedroom and pulled a large brown suitcase out from under the bed. There, laid out like four fat black puddings, were Junky's offspring, and Junky herself promptly jumped in and proceeded to give them their afternoon tea. Penelope Ann glowed with love and pride and was completely impervious to the incongruity of the situation.

"They just cannot stay here!" I protested in horror.

"Why ever not?" she questioned in amazement.

"It's an impossible set-up," I declared. "You will have to give them away or else have them put to sleep."

"However could you be so cruel!" she cried in horror. "Would you give your children away or have them put to sleep?"

Not for the first time since Penelope Ann came to stay, I felt that I was walking up a stairs and some of the steps were missing. A few days afterwards the conductor on the Bandon bus must have felt the same way when Penelope Ann boarded his bus with a shopping bag overflowing with pups, their mother following on a lead.

That weekend I had a phone call from a lady who introduced herself as Penelope Ann's mother. She seemed a charming person and fully aware of what an unusual young woman her daughter was. In the course of the conversation I asked her why Penelope Ann was so far away from her family.

"She likes Ireland," her mother answered, "and being slightly eccentric, as Penelope Ann is, does not seem to pose such a problem in Ireland."

I was not sure if that was a compliment to our tolerance or a confirmation of our daftness; I was certainly beginning to feel that I was losing my grip. "She likes it with you," the mother continued, "but she won't stay much longer. She prefers to move on."

I had begun to think that she would never go and that my lovely flat would be turned into a kennel for mongrels. But one day, just as the pups were getting mobile and able to jump out of the suitcase, she knocked on the kitchen door.

"I'm moving on," she said.

"Where are you going?" I asked with relief.

"To a guest-house in Cork," she informed me. "Will you drive me in tomorrow."

"Certainly," I said.

Our car was in the garage for repairs and we had on loan a shabby green van which looked as if it might best be used for selling carpets door to door. The front passenger door was jammed, so all goods and passengers had to get in through the back door. The following day, with Penelope Ann calling instructions over my shoulder, I drove up in front of a gracious, imposing house which was to be her next abode. I wondered how many details she had given her future hosts, or, more important still, what she had decided not to tell them. As we braked to a halt a tall, distinguished-looking, grey-haired man came down the steps smiling. The smile froze on his face when, having left the driver's seat, I opened the back door of the van and a procession emerged slowly. First Junky jumped out, wagging her tail in confident anticipation of a warm welcome. Then came one of my children, clasping two pups, and after him my sad-faced seven-year-old holding his favourite pup. Next out was the fourth pup and finally Penelope Ann, resplendent in a floppy red hat. The man's face was a picture of astonishment.

"My God! Is there any more in there?" he asked me in amazement.

Penelope Ann took over with a flourish. Holding out her hand as if she were a visiting royal conferring on him a rare and wonderful honour, she announced in her most toffee-nosed accent, "I am Penelope Ann Carter Page, and I have come to stay."

The Village Shopkeeper

WHEN JACKY GOT his first heart-attack he was told to take it easy, but he could never be turned into a slow-moving person. Slim, fit and agile, he got things done while others were still thinking about them. Behind his counter he combined economy of movement, efficient service and a pleasant disposition. When his customers' shopping bags were full he folded his arms on his side of the counter as they did likewise on theirs, and proceeded to discuss the state of the village, the parish, the country, and sometimes perhaps the world, but nearest to his heart was the state of the GAA.

After a conversation with Jacky a person felt that life was good; he passed his joy of living on to them. Everybody, no matter what their station in life, was equal in his eyes. People did not always think as he did, of course. Once we had a titled lady living in the area who insisted on being addressed with all her handles attached. When one of the locals remarked that there was no way that he was going to do this, Jacky replied equably, "Sure if it keeps her happy, it's no skin off your nose." While he moved easily amongst people, he loved to have fun with the children. He gave them penny bars and lollipops and they came to him for ice-cream because his was the most generous cut of all.

Every morning he ran around the village, popping the morning papers in through the letter-boxes, and in the evening he did the same thing when the bus had brought the *Evening Echo*. Old people who could not make it to the shop had their bread and milk delivered. Telling him to slow down was like trying to stop a mountain stream from flowing; quick-thinking by nature, his movements matched his mental agility.

It sometimes worried me when I watched him shifting crates full of bottles in the shop and pushing his wheelbarrow around the garden. I mentioned it to the doctor who over the years had proved a good friend and shrewd doctor, combining humanity with medical expertise in his advice.

"Well, Alice," he said, "you can't make an invalid out of him. If you take his independence you'll kill him in another way."

I knew he was right and from then on I stopped trying to put a brake on Jacky, much to his relief. One evening as we were both tidying up the shop after a busy day we lifted crates together. At the time I was recovering from flu and looking at me he grinned and said, "Alice, the two of us together would make one good fellow."

As old age slowed him down slightly he withdrew gradually from the shop and spent more and more time in his much-loved garden. All the same, he continued to come into the shop in the evenings when it was quiet to meet his old friends. Every night they had an endless supply of stories to tell one another, but the group was dwindling as some had gone on to higher places.

He went every morning to Mass and sometimes if I came on him unawares in a quiet corner of the house or garden he would be kneeling in silent prayer. For him there was no gap between morning Mass and daily life. Only somebody in spiritual communion with a higher level could have been filled with the joy of living which Jacky had.

The second heart-attack came in the middle of a freezing cold November night. When Aunty Peg called from the foot of the stairs to come quickly, we knew that it had to be serious. Jacky was lying back against the pillows white-faced and shaken. The doctor came and sent him to hospital right away. As Gabriel drove him in I sat with Peg while the grey dawn seeped in the window of their living-room. We both knew that there was no comparison between this heart-attack and the one several years earlier. That had been only a rumble; this was the full earthquake. Gabriel came back and tried to make a bad story sound as good as possible. He told me later that Jacky had said on the way to the hospital, "If God took me now I would be happy to go." But God did not take him. He hovered between life and death for a few days; then, on the evening that he recovered consciousness, his first question was: "Did Cork win the match?" They had played in the national league that Sunday and he had not heard the result.

He was in hospital for six months and the nuns who cared for him could not have been kinder. Every night when we went to see him I marvelled at his capacity to endure pain cheerfully. When I heard the news that the surgeon had been forced to make a decision to amputate his leg to prevent gangrene I dreaded the effect the news would have on him, but he was still his old happy self and I came home feeling better than I had been going in. He was giving comfort rather than asking for it.

During this trauma Aunty Peg suffered with him but despite this she never lost her sense of humour. She did not like being on her own so one of our children slept in Jacky's bed. In their long, narrow bedroom over the shop, which had lovely old furniture that a friend who was a cabinet-maker had made for them, Aunty Peg taught Sean the names of all the saints in the rows of holy pictures that lined the walls. She herself seldom went to visit Jacky as she did not like hospitals, but she wrote to him every day. No matter how depressing the news from the hospital, she never gave up hope. Her friends from all around the village visited her regularly and drank tea with her, or something stronger if that was to their liking.

Eventually Jacky came home with an artificial leg and two crutches. It was terrible to see this man who had always moved as nimbly as a mountain goat now slowed almost to a standstill by this heavy, awkward artificial leg. The weight of it was incredible; it pinned him to the ground. But Peg was absolutely thrilled to have him home. Steps were a problem, so he slept in the little front room that had a window opening onto the street, and in the early morning he could watch from his bed the people passing by. It was summer then, so during the day he sat out in the garden where he read all the papers while his little dog Topsy stretched out in the shade beneath the garden seat. There was a general election campaign in full swing, and the political wrangling, the count and the post mortems that followed all passed away the time for him as he had lost none of his interest in politics.

The artificial limb was awkward and cumbersome and though Jacky must have found his limited mobility very frustrating he did not complain. He was scheduled to go to the remedial clinic in Dún Laoghaire for special training and he hoped that he would achieve a certain measure of flexibility which would give him back some of his independence. The call came in late July. Gabriel was to drive him up but at the last minute Aunty Peg said to me, "Alice, why don't you go with him?" We set out on a warm sunny morning for Dublin. As we debated where we would stop for lunch I realised for the first time the problem steps present to the disabled. We sat around the table laughing and chatting, and I could almost convince myself that we were having a day out together, but our arrival in Dún Laoghaire in the late afternoon brought me back to reality. The visit to that clinic was a chastening experience for it was a world where brave people swam against the tide.

We settled Jacky in and said goodbye to him in the dining-room where he sat having tea with people who had far greater limitations on their freedom than he. As I held his hand he looked up at me, and there in his eyes I saw for the first time his suffering and fears, and his sadness that we were going home and leaving him there alone. As I walked out the door my eyes were blinded with tears.

During the week that followed we got a cheery letter nearly

every day, assuring us that he was doing well and mastering the leg. Everybody in the village was interested in his progress and called to see Aunty Peg, bolstering her belief in his recovery. Fr Seamus called regularly but cautioned me: "Don't expect too much." Aunty Peg and I wrote to him daily and posted on the Cork papers. We painted the house as a surprise for his return, and Gabriel planned to visit him on the Sunday when he was up for the All-Ireland Final in which Cork was playing.

At 7 a.m. on Friday morning the phone call came. He had died peacefully in his sleep during the night. When I heard the news my mind could hardly absorb it. My first thought was of Aunty Peg. How were we to tell her? As it was early we decided to let her sleep on. I went out to the guest-house to get the breakfast for the guests, my mind in a turmoil. I put three trays of rashers one after the other under the grill and burned each one. One of my friends came into the kitchen and took over.

When Aunty Peg got up I went in as she was having her breakfast and told her as gently as I could. Her first reaction was to cry, "Oh, no, no," and then she looked at me sadly and said, "After all he went through: to think that it should come to this." But I learned that day that the old can be far more resilient than the young. The news went around the village and the neighbours who during the previous weeks had come to encourage now poured in all through the day to bring comfort. Aunty Peg proved to be amazingly strong, and the companionship of old friends helped to ease her pain. On such occasions people certainly need others. Old friends laughed and cried with Aunty Peg as they swopped funny and sad stories of Jacky's years in their village shop. But most of all they recalled his kindness. With tears in her eyes one woman said to me, "God bless him, but he kept food on many a table including my own when times were hard, and often he was never paid for it, but no one ever knew."

The following day we drove to Dún Laoghaire with the local

undertaker and some friends to bring Jacky home. We were taken into the little mortuary chapel where he was laid out. Since I had heard of his death I had had an ache inside in me, but when I saw him the pain eased. He had a smile on his face and looked as if he had just heard good news. How could we be sad when he looked so joyful? Aunty Peg came out of the mortuary looking more at peace, and I thought to myself that he was helping us still.

Waiting for us in Dún Laoghaire were people who had connections with our village. Some were old natives of Innishannon who were now living in Dublin; others' parents had come from the village and they themselves had often come back on holidays. All had been contacted by relatives from home and it was heart-warming to meet them.

As we drove home through the various towns it was strangely comforting to see people bless themselves as the hearse passed by. Prior to that I had never really thought about it. Arriving home was a very touching experience. At the entrance to the village the Valley Rovers lined both sides of the street. Weather-beaten country men who had played with him, younger men whom he had sometimes cheered to victory, and young lads whose hurleys he had often banded and to whom he had given penny bars stood together in respect. They walked along beside the hearse through the village and up the hill to our little church, where Fr Seamus was waiting to welcome him home. Inside the front porch his old friend Ellie, the chapel woman, was there to signal her altar boys to toll his home-coming bell.

When we came back from the church the house was packed with neighbours and far-flung relatives. Aunty Peg surprised me afterwards by remembering exactly who was there – and even who was not and should have been. Despite her sorrow, and her exhaustion after the long journey, she still had a spark of her old humour. She looked down the length of the dining-room at a cousin whom she had never really liked, and said to me with a tired smile on her pale face, "Would you look at the hat on that one. Isn't it time she had more sense, at this hour of her life!"

The following morning I awoke with the dawn and went out into Jacky's garden. It was full of dew, sunshine and singing birds. Going up past the old apple-tree, I sat on a stone with my back against the hen-house and soaked in the warmth and peace. The hens clucked as they woke up on their perches behind me. Here in close harmony with God and nature Jacky had developed a deep inner peace which he had exuded in a warm love of his fellow human-beings. His death had been a release from his suffering but his spirit was still here in the beauty he had created. White butterflies drifted along between the flowers and as the tears ran down my face I knew that I was experiencing a moment when the division between the here and the hereafter was very thin.

Later that morning in a graveyard filled with sunshine and people we laid him to rest, surrounded by his old friends above and beside him. As the white butterflies fluttered around the yew trees I watched Aunty Peg's bowed figure heave in sorrow, and wondered how she would cope with life without him, or how we could fill for her the gap his going had left. Then somewhere in my mind on that warm August day he let me know that he would be waiting, and that the wait would not be long.

Later that day Cork won the All-Ireland Final. From where he surely watched with delight, Jacky did not need a stand ticket.

Friends and Neighbours

To JACKY DEATH was nothing to be afraid of, but for Aunty Peg it was a different matter. Soon after his death she began to feel unwell, so the doctor sent her into hospital for tests. She hated every minute of it, and objected vehemently to all the injections and tubes that were part of hospital routine. Finally she could tolerate it no longer and, having always been her own woman, she discharged herself and came home, much to the annoyance of the consultant and matron. That day she sat by the fire in her sitting-room and told me, "I'm not going back into that hospital. If I'm going to die it's going to be here in the comfort of my own home."

I sought out the doctor for advice. "Well," he said, "she has cancer and it is fairly advanced. They could operate but there are no guarantees, and if she wants to stay at home she should have that choice."

"Will she suffer?" I asked.

"Not with proper medical care, and I'll be here when she needs me."

He was as good as his word, and during the months that followed proved to be a tower of strength.

In the beginning Aunty Peg came down the narrow high stairs behind the shop every day to sit by her sitting-room fire. She wrote dozens of letters to people who had written to her since Jacky's death. At night one of our children slept with her, but as she gradually grew weaker she could no longer get out of bed by herself, and I changed places with Sean.

The time that followed was a very lonely, disturbing, sometimes sad experience, but strange as it may seem, there were

116

times, too, which were very funny. She was a great patient, which made caring for her very easy, but she did not want to die and this on occasions caused me real distress. On a bad day she would ask me plaintively, "Am I going to die?" and I could never tell her because the following day she might be feeling in better spirits and talking about going to the wood for a walk when she was better. I did not want to take the joy of those good days from her while she still had them. It was almost as if she did not want to know.

And yet, as she grew weaker, part of her did know. But she did not want to discuss it. One night she instructed me to open the tall press in her bedroom. "Take out the parcel on the top shelf," she told me. I did as I was asked and laid it on the bed where we opened it. Inside was a pair of white linen sheets, pillow-cases edged with lace, and a heavy crochet bedspread. "You know what they are for?" she asked. I nodded silently, wrapped them up and put them back in the press. I sat on her bed wondering if she wanted to say anything more, but she caught my hand and said, "We'll let it at that."

She never mentioned the bedclothes for her wake again, but from then on we both knew, and understood that she did not want to talk about her approaching death.

Again her relatives and friends came to see her. One well-meaning lady, however, annoyed her intensely.

"Peg," she would gush, "you are looking wonderful!"

When she left Peg would look at me with a knowing smile on her face. "Does she think that I am a pure fool? I know well how I look." Another, much wiser visitor brought her brandy, and every night before settling down she would smile and say, "We'll have a drop." I would pour two glasses. "Sláinte," she would say raising her glass. "If I don't die soon you'll be an alcoholic!"

Her long, narrow bedroom had a window that opened onto the garden at the back and another that opened to the street at the front. All her life she had needed very little sleep and had often passed hours of the night looking out the window. Now, even though she could no longer stand or walk, she continued to get out of bed and was in danger of falling on the floor. She could not understand why she could not walk because in her dreams, which she mixed up with reality, she had no difficulty in walking. She would wake up after a long sleep and tell me that she had been on a farm outside the village, a place which she had perhaps visited regularly years previously. Then in surprise she would ask me, "How is it I can walk around the fields over there and I cannot walk at all here?" Her mind began to wander and went way back to the days of her girlhood. Sometimes she thought that her dead relatives were all around the room, especially Jacky, and she would ask me if I could see them. Gradually the memory of Jacky faded, and it was her parents and her early childhood that she spoke about. Childhood hurts long forgotten and buried in the deep recesses of her mind came to the surface.

It was my first experience of caring for a dying person, and I found it mentally draining. She had lost touch with this world and in some strange way I felt that I, too, was going along with her. It gave me a sense of release to leave the room and come downstairs and cross the garden to hear the children laughing and shouting in our kitchen. Their youthful energy revitalised me, and sustained me against the malaise of death in the sickroom. Their attitude to her illness was interesting to see. The two teenagers were obviously shaken and dismayed by the change in Aunty Peg, while the younger ones bounced in and out of her room as if everything was normal.

During those months our friends and neighbours were wonderful. They visited and cooked but most important of all they took time to talk and sit with her. At Christmas one friend brought a large supply of mincepies; the children were especially thrilled because it had seemed that they were going to have a pie-less Christmas. When we had a power failure during a very cold spell in January, one old man brought his gas heater and tank of gas up the stairs to keep her room warm. Up the street was the lady whom we called the Nurse, and she came some evenings and sat for a few hours, as did another retired lady who was an old friend of Peg's. Another friend, Betsy, also sat with her during the evening. At the time we had a marvellous girl called Ann working in the shop. She was always willing to help and when we had to leave the room during the day she ran up and down the stairs to check that everything was all right. It was a great mental ease to us, because always on our minds was the worry that Aunty Peg would fall out of bed. While it happened occasionally, thankfully she never hurt herself. Nevertheless, whenever I ran upstairs after a short absence I was always apprehensive that something could have gone wrong while I had been away. Even when we were not in the room with her she was still in our minds. The security of having somebody to sit with her was a tremendous relief. Only her friends could stay with her; it would have been difficult to introduce into her room anybody who was not already close to her. She herself only wanted around her people whom she knew well and loved. She had always been a religious person in the sense of performing her religious duties regularly, but with death approaching she cast aside all the trappings of religion as if they brought her no comfort. Her face lit up though when Gabriel came into the room, to sit on the bed and hold her hand. She needed love more than prayers now.

Waiting for this slow, inevitable death had a strangely hypnotic effect on me. It was almost like standing on the beach watching the tide come relentlessly nearer, waiting for a wave to wash over her and take her away. Sometimes I wished that it would just come and that there would be an end to it; then I was flooded with guilt to have even had such a thought. Because she did not want to die she was like someone hanging from a cliff by her finger-tips; afraid to let go, she held on desperately, even as her grip weakened. I had this extraordinary feeling that I was holding her: if I let go, she would fall; if I did not, I would go with her. From long hours together in that room we were both slightly outside the ordinary world then. Her room had become the focus of my life.

One grey day in March I reviewed the situation with the doctor. He came regularly and was a great comfort. Because she was used to me and we understood each other well I did not want to upset Aunty Peg by getting anybody else in to stay with her at night, but if the present situation continued it would have to be done. "How long more will it go on?" I asked the doctor. I felt guilty even to be voicing the question because it made me feel that I was wishing her death closer. But he answered, "It will be all over before the week is out." As in everything about her illness he was right. She would sleep for long periods but would wake at times and be perfectly lucid for a few minutes. One day she asked me for her jewellery box, and having looked at the different pieces she smiled and went back to sleep. Another day she looked at me and said, "When you came here first I did not like you. I thought you were young and silly with daft ideas," and she smiled with a spark of her old humour.

Gradually the periods of sleep grew longer and one wet evening when a cold wind whipped the rain against the small windows she slipped into a coma. Fr Seamus, who had come regularly to visit her, said the prayers for the dying and anointed her. I wondered if she could still hear us. Gabriel and the two younger children gathered around the bed. The two older ones had opted not to be there and we felt that it should be their own choice. Sean, who was ten, had always been particularly close to her; he touched her face and arranged her well-worn rosary beads between her fingers. I hoped that she could feel him near. As the night wore on her breathing became more laboured. While her niece, Agnes, came and sat with her, I went to the bed in the next room and dreamed of falling over a high cliff.

It took Aunty Peg a long time to die and it was very distressing to listen and watch. Betsy came and was far more supportive than I, and then the Nurse came and brought with her an air of serene capability because she had sat at many a death-bed around the parish. She was wonderful and soothing both to the woman in the bed and the one standing weakly beside it. When the laboured breathing gasped to a halt at midday it was a welcome release. Quietness filled the long, low room as life slowly whispered away, and a great peace came over Aunty Peg and indeed over me. I felt drained of vitality, as if some of my inner being had gone with her. An absolute stillness filled every corner of the room.

Walking down the stairs and opening the door into her sitting-room the finality of death hit me. I realised that all the little things which she had treasured and cared for all her life were now left behind, and that she would never again sit here where she had spent most of her days. Standing in this quiet room on that cold day I was aware of how final death was. It was no great truth I had discovered, but it was the first time that I had realised it in the marrow of my bones.

Later Gabriel and I wrapped her in a blanket and carried her through the garden full of daffodils to the front room of the guest-house where she was to be laid out convenient to the street and the people coming in for the wake. While the Nurse and Betsy laid her out I brought in big bunches of the daffodils that she had always loved and arranged them around her bed between the lighted candles. Now it was her turn to use the shining brass candlesticks which had travelled around the village to different wakes over the years. She had always kept them polished and gleaming, ready for anybody who needed them. Her bed was dressed with the bed-linen and crochet bedspread which she had shown me months before.

We wondered how the children would react to what had happened when they came home from school. I took the two younger ones into the candle-lit room. They looked at Aunty Peg in silence for a few minutes and then Sean took the rosary beads that were entwined around her fingers and said, "That's the wrong rosary beads. She told me that she wanted the old black ones when she was laid out. I'll get it now." He ran out of the room and returned with her old rosary beads. They had obviously discussed all these details, much to my surprise. Diarmuid, aged seven, promptly went out and collected all his friends from around the village and made them kneel and say their prayers, and threatened them that they were not to laugh as this was a very serious occasion. But though they did not laugh, I certainly smiled as he stood in front of his row of mourners and watched over them sternly.

Because she had been part of the place for so long it was fitting that Aunty Peg's wake should take place in the middle of the village. Because she had died in the afternoon the wake continued until the following evening. There was a constant flow of people through the house. Many of the neighbours sat through the night quietly chatting, and as the news spread around the parish her old friends came to say goodbye. It was a peaceful farewell in the end.

Mature Motherhood

THERE IS NO such thing as the perfect mother, because motherhood calls for the stamina of youth allied to the wisdom of age. I had had four children with nothing but the stamina of youth to sustain me. When I became pregnant soon after Aunty Peg's death I learned what the state of motherhood was like when, if not actually blessed by the wisdom of old age, it was at least made more resilient by the cushion of maturity.

Children, I believed, reached a civilised level of behaviour when you could sit them all down at the dinner table without wondering when the youngest member was going to upset a plate on top of an unsuspecting visitor or turn a sauce-boat sideways with a misdirected elbow. That year when our youngest got his First Holy Communion we went out for lunch. Up to then we had always celebrated family occasions at home, where we were joined by Jacky and Peg. Now they were gone, and their absence would be less noticeable away from familiar surroundings. We had a great day and I felt that I had reached a milestone on the road of motherhood. I was pleased with my progress but a little sad to be celebrating, as we thought, our final First Holy Communion.

After discovering my pregnant condition we wondered how the children would react to the news. We decided to furnish them with early details so that we could all walk the path of my pregnancy together. The two young ones were absolutely delighted. The news that we were going to have a new baby was as exciting to them as getting a new puppy; the only problem was that they wanted it immediately. With a big smile spreading over his face one of the teenagers remarked, "Wonders will never cease!" The other one grinned at me and said, "God, Mom! I though that you were gone past it." With all these varying reactions tucked under my expanding belt I wondered how a new baby would fit into this all-male household. As things turned out, instead of one man telling me to take it easy and to put my feet up, I now had five, and was treated like the Queen Mother. I decided that as this would probably be my pregnant swan-song I was going to enjoy it.

Babies and I had the habit of parting company ahead of schedule, so I was ready for Christmas that year weeks in advance. In the event I just made it past Christmas and went into the nursing home on St Stephen's night. As I lay in the labour ward I thought how much had changed since my first visit. Then the place had bustled with activity: rushing nurses, complaining women, rolling trolleys, hurrying doctors, an occasional infant wail. Now all was quiet. I seemed to have the entire floor to myself. The baby boom was well and truly over.

Very few births can be described as painless but this was as near as made no difference. When the gynaecologist held up the baby my first question was, "Is he all right?"

"Fine," he answered, "but it's not a boy, it's a girl."

I was so thrilled that I cried with joy. I could have danced all the way home and back again. The whole country was in the grip of a freezing blizzard, and it took Gabriel four hours to make the journey from home, but for me it was a golden day filled with happiness. The next member of the family I saw was my eldest son, who called to the nursing home on his way home from football training. When he heard the news his face lit up with delight. "Well done, Mom," he said, and clapped me on the back as if I had won a county final.

When the baby arrived home she was the centre of attention. Prior to her birth we had wondered how we would feel about the return of nappies and night feeds, but we had not realised then all the help that was available with grown-up children around. I decided that mature motherhood had a lot to recommend it.

Changing Times

THE TIME HAD come to open a new chapter in village shopping and close an old chapter in our lives. The traditional village shop was no longer able to meet the needs of our changing society. With our entry into the EEC the Irish economy had been boosted and land prices and wages had taken a jump. There was more money and confidence in circulation and people's tastes were becoming more sophisticated. Increasing specialisation in land management meant that many farmers no longer found it viable to grow their own potatoes and vegetables or to keep their own hens. The days of the farmers killing their own pigs and growing their own cabbage to boil with the bacon were fast disappearing. Instead of producing for themselves they now joined the shopping queues.

The villagers had given up tilling their own ground and the hen-houses disappeared from the bottoms of gardens. Mass-production in specialised units made vegetables cheaper to buy than to grow. People no longer baked their own bread, and a huge selection of conveyor-belt bread and cakes came on the market. Instant and frozen foods began to take over from the slower traditional methods of cooking. There was more money available for luxuries and a bigger supply and display of well-packaged goods created needs we never knew we had. Because customers now paid cash at the check-out, instead of the old system where customers kept an account, goods could be sold cheaper, which made for more satisfied customers.

People were leaving the village to shop in the new supermarkets in Cork so the time had come, we felt, to provide one at home. To do this would require a huge financial invest-

ment. Though we had recovered from our previous development we did not have anything like the resources needed to
turn a small village shop into a large supermarket, with all
the additional shelving and refrigeration that was necessary.
When we had embarked on our first major bout of construc-
tion we had run right up against a credit squeeze at the
banks; now, incredibly, the same thing happened again.

We went to the bank manager cap in hand and, after
gloomy forecasts about how impossible it was to get loans, he
promised to apply to head office and let us know the response
in due course.

As soon as the baby was sleeping through the night and
winter had disappeared over the horizon, we started work on
the new supermarket. We had moved by now into the corner
house, so we were finally ensconced under one roof. The
corner house was no longer a guest-house though some of it
was still in flats. As a home it was large and rambling, so
everybody had more space – which was a big bonus when
small boys were growing into leggy teenagers.

Taking down the old house was sad in many ways and
stripping rooms where generations of a family had lived was
a strange experience. Little family treasures materially
worthless but sentimentally valuable could not be thrown
away, and yet we could not keep everything. The walls that
Aunty Peg and I had painted a rich red in preparation for
Jacky's home-coming; the small room in which he had slept
when he could not climb the stairs; the fireplace beside which
our first-born had taken his first step – these were all going.
We were pulling down corners which stored many memories,
but the one I regretted most was Jacky's rose garden where
his rambling roses draped over wooden fences. It was the
price that had to be paid for survival: the days of the small
village shop were gone. But one tree that was in a very
vulnerable position close to the back wall of the new building
survived.

Years previously Jacky and I had looked down at that little

holly tree and he had said, "In time to come, Alice, ye will extend back here because ye will have to. I will be gone then, but try to save this tree. It takes a holly tree a long time to grow, and it would be good if it survived."

By the time we extended the tree had grown above my head and I was determined that it would survive. When Tony, who was levelling the site, manoeuvred his bulldozer around the tall holly he said to me in frustration. "Missus, this would be a lot easier but for your bloody tree!" But I remembered Jacky's words and dug my heels in. A few years afterwards I had to dig them in again when a fussy hygiene inspector decided that the tree was too close to the door of the butchery department. He said to me, "I think that tree should go." I looked him straight in the eye and said, "Over my dead body."

During the months that it took to build the supermarket I sometimes thought that my dead body would be found in the foundations. But Gabriel had always been one to tackle large obstacles with single-minded determination, and we had learned a lot from our previous experience. We now knew that nobody delivered when they said they would and that if you thought that something was going to cost one hundred pounds it finished up costing two hundred and fifty. Luckily our old friends Jerry and Davey were back with us, and because they were great workers the walls rose around us as fast as if we had had twice the workforce. In front of a thick plastic sheet the old shop still functioned in a state of dusty chaos. Gabriel divided his energies between both departments and the children helped after school and at weekends. They mixed concrete, drew blocks and measured lengths of timber under Jerry's fast and impatient directions. It was a case of all hands on deck: even the baby sat in her pram and watched with interest.

Into the midst of all this muddy progress the bank dropped a bombshell. No loan. By then we had no back wall to the old shop and the roof had been taken off. It became my job to keep the bank manager quiet. I had my work cut out for me! One day as I sat outside his office, waiting to get a roasting about the condition of our account, I took out my notebook and wrote:

Is there anything more intimidating than sitting on a hard chair outside a bank manager's office, waiting to be interrogated as to why your account is overdrawn? It is a warm, sunny Thursday morning and it should be a bright, happy day full of freedom. Instead I sit here bound by financial fetters. They are squeezing the relaxation and bounce out of me. Do I lack the confidence to see over these constricting pounds? Because this problem will pass. Money, or rather the lack of it, should not in anyone's world be capable of such a belittling effect. Why do we have such financial boundaries in our world? Boundaries that tower above us, threatening to bury or at least to choke us with the dust that rises when they collapse. If it never happens we will have suffered in dread expectancy. Could it be ...

And so I ended my speculation because the bank manager's door opened. That note was a page from a chapter in my life when the bank manager was a regular correspondent and Saturdays and Sundays were days of peace because he could not ring. But sometimes you don't realise how well-off you are until things get worse. A few weeks later the tax man decided to brighten up our lives with a demand for back tax from Jacky's time, for an amount that, had he been alive, would certainly have given him a heart-attack.

We sat in a hollow surrounded by financial hills. If we sat too long and thought about them they would bury us. All we could do was to keep our sights set on our goal, and know that one day we would rise above the problem. So began a long, slow financial climb.

Apart from the financial pressure it was a challenging, exciting time and it had its lighter moments. When the wall behind the post office had to be taken down we put everything pertaining to the post office counter into a large cardboard box. A sprightly, titled Englishman who lived locally came in and enquired in his beautiful accent, "I say, where is the post office gone?" I pointed to the cardboard box. "Well, my dear," he said, peering into the box, "we have certainly got a post office that's different. The Royal Mail never saw the likes of this!"

Gradually out of this confusion came order. The ceramic tile floor was laid, dangling electric wires were tidied up, refrigeration was installed and shelves were stacked with goods. At six o' clock on the night before our official opening just one thing was missing: we had no front door and no windows. We promised to be the first supermarket in Ireland to be opened without a front door! They should have been fitted the previous week – "We'll be there tomorrow," the suppliers had promised faithfully – but now we had four holes in the wall and not a pane of glass to cover them. We were stocking shelves and time was ticking away, but still no windows and doors came. I made frantic phone calls, spitting fire and thunder. Finally at 10 p.m. they arrived. At 3 a.m. the fitters left. The windows were in, the front doors were swinging, but all were in need of a good cleaning. As I washed the windows at about four o'clock on a mellow October morning a lone motorist drove past. He slowed to a halt and reversed back. He had a good look at me, blessed himself, and drove away.

The official opening was performed by Jacky's sister, Molly. She was the link between the old and the new because she had been born in the original house where the supermarket now stood. All the village people gathered around the door, and the tiredness and tensions fell away from us as we stood there surrounded by our friends and neighbours who were all so pleased for us. We drank champagne and a wonderful feeling of euphoria stole over us. The supermarket was blessed by Fr Seamus. When he requested holy water I ran into the kitchen knowing that after the confusion of the previous months I would not be able to find any. I turned on the tap, filled a bottle, shook the salt-cellar into it and on my way back along the corridor asked the Lord to make it holy.

One final thing worried us. We did not want our supermarket to lose completely the atmosphere of the old village shop and become impersonally efficient. If this happened we would lose some of the flavour of our village life. But the village style filled the new surroundings just as it had the old. People chatted along the aisles and called greetings to their friends. In a small place, shopping was more than the acquiring of goods; it was an opportunity to meet the neighbours. These people's personalities did not give much chance for standardisation to take hold. Some of the customers were wonderful company. One day I was chatting with a local man and he asked me where he could find the tea. "Stay where you are," I said helpfully, "and I'll get it for you. What kind do you want – Barry's?"

"For God's sake," he answered, "you don't expect me to drink Coalition tea!" Even tea could have a political flavour. Other goods were flavoured, too, by the accent people gave them. At the time we had in the butchery department cartons containing two small chickens each. A man who lived up the street came to buy a pair of these chickens but discovered there was only one left in the carton. He pointed at the lone chicken: "Where is the other little hoor gone?" he demanded.

So we settled down to run the supermarket and even though the work was hard the customers made it interesting. We always appreciated the people who shopped with us and but for them another facet of village life would have died out. Some of the other shops in the village were owned by old people and remained unchanged, but when the owners died they closed down. One of these was the little sweet shop up the hill where Ellie and Nonie lived.

The Chapel Woman

OLD MRS MCCARTHY had been the chapel woman all her life, and when she died her daughter Nonie took over, regarding it as a family inheritance rather than a job. Nonie carried around in her head the history of the graveyard which surrounded the church. She knew who was buried in every corner, even those who had left no address or who lay beneath the small rock-like marking stones without inscriptions. These marking stones were the forerunner of headstones; people knew their family graves by measuring the distance of these rocks from each other, from the nearby church, or even from the nearest ditch.

She was a soft-spoken, stooped little lady who arranged weddings, funerals and christenings, and she was a reference book on all church events past and present. She did everything but say Mass and hear confessions – though with her in-depth knowledge of the parish she probably had a good idea of what went on in the confessionals as well. She did the church laundry and counted the collections. The village shops and pubs came to her for change, so the brown pennies collected on Sunday often found their way back during the following week to their original owners.

To supplement her income she looked after the dispensary, and she had a little sweet shop simply called "Nonie's", which was so small that it could be filled by just one customer. The children on their way up and down to school popped in and out to her clutching their pennies. The cream-coloured counter topped with a piece of frayed brown lino was very high, and Nonie's customers were very small, so she recognised them all by the tops of their heads. To the left of her slatted front door was one small window packed with jars and flat boxes of all kinds of sweets. The children pressed their faces against the glass while making their selections, their heads blocking the light and darkening the little shop. They squeezed inside and bartered at the counter, then left with strings of Black Jack hanging from their jaws and sticks of Peggy's Leg clenched between their teeth like long white cigars. They bought hard penny-bars and fists of Cleeves toffees that gave hours of sticky sucking for one penny.

As she grew older Nonie became crippled with arthritis. Her older sister Ellie came back to look after her and to take over all her duties. But while small, frail Nonie seemed bowed beneath the weight of her responsibilities, Ellie was a big woman who took everything in her stride. Nonie regarded her church work as an inherited honour while to Ellie it was something that circumstances had thrust upon her. Nothing excited her. Christenings, funerals, weddings, parish priests and bishops all blew across her path, but she continued on her original course with calm determination.

As the years went by many new houses were built around the parish. Church and dispensary activity increased, making Ellie's job busier. Nonie's condition deteriorated so that she ended up in a wheelchair, but still Ellie carried on cheerfully. Though over eighty years of age she looked far younger, having about her none of the usual frailties of old age. She was tall, solid and upright, and had a pleasant, broad face crowned with a fine head of brown curly hair streaked with grey. The only thing to mark the passage of time was that she was very deaf, but even this you would be totally unaware of if you did not know her well. She had the happy knack of guiding the conversation along her own lines; if you said something to her she nodded smilingly, and you never quite knew if she had heard you or not. She said very little but her expressions and nods were comments in themselves, and Ellie was the only person I ever knew who could carry on a conversation without opening her mouth. When something annoyed her, though, she was very forthright in her opinions. Though she was not one to display her emotions easily, her broad face glowed when the church was alive with flowers for a wedding. She loved fresh flowers, and at a funeral she would sigh at the sight of plastic wreaths.

She was aware of everything that went on in the village, but kept her own counsel. She lined up the children for First Holy Communion and kept the altar boys in their place. When the hearse came up the hill bringing a parishioner to the church, she stood in the front porch like a one-woman guard of honour and her altar boys stood ready to toll the bell. There was about her an absolute regularity and dependability. Every morning she went to open the church for early morning Mass. She never rushed but walked along at an even pace. After Mass she opened the sweet shop for the children on their way to school and later came down the hill to open the dispensary for the doctor. In between these trips she found time to look after Nonie.

She cared for the ailing Nonie with kindness but with great firmness. Nonie's mind was inclined to wander but Ellie jerked her back to reality. Some evenings Nonie would have the table set for three when Ellie came in, and Ellie would demand: "Who's that extra place for?"

"That's for Jack," Nonie would answer.

"For God's sake," Ellie would declare in exasperation, "Jack is above in the graveyard for the last twenty years: he's hardly going to come down for his tea!"

Ellie's firmness held Nonie in the real world for years when she might have slipped into confusion. Ellie was not one to pay lip-service to her duties but carried them out unswervingly because in her world life had its responsibilities and you looked after your own. Though advanced in years she carried a workload that would have exhausted a far younger woman. When I remarked to her on her amazing stamina she smiled in amusement and said matter-of-factly, "One day I will drop down stone cold dead, and that will be that."

Fr Seamus had great respect for her, and of all the priests

that she had worked with he was her favourite. Not, of course, that she ever said so; indeed she treated him like a wayward son. Once when he had arrived back from holidays she said to me: "He's back now but I'm not going to pretend that he is by asking him if he enjoyed his holiday, because he did not think it worth his while to tell me that he was going." He had told her all right, but she had not heard him.

From the time she took over the duties of chapel woman she never missed a morning opening the church on time. But one morning she was not there, and we knew that something had to be very wrong. She had got a very bad pain in her leg during the night and Fr Seamus had taken her into hospital. Her departure caused repercussions around the village. There was nobody to open the dispensary, the children were surprised to find their sweet shop closed, Nonie had no one to care for her and the parish was without someone to keep track of all the comings and goings to do with the church.

The doctor procured a bed for Nonie in the nearby cottage hospital until Ellie was back in circulation again. Two of the neighbours tidied the sisters' house in preparation for their return. Fr Seamus had gone to see Ellie a few times that day and reported great progress, but later that night when he went in to see her she died quite suddenly. Because he had great affection for the stalwart old lady who had soldiered with him for so many years, the Mass he said for her the following morning was a celebration of love and the church was filled with her presence. She and her family had been one of the mainstays of village life for many years, and with her going the door of the little sweet shop closed for good. The following day when we laid her to rest in her family plot behind the church, one of the wreaths placed there by her old friend Mrs Hawkins, who prayed in the other church in the village, bore a fitting epitaph for Ellie: "Well done, thou good and faithful servant." Shortly afterwards Nonie died too. The tradition of the dedicated chapel woman who regarded her work as a vocation rather than a job had come to an end.

They Were Great Women

SHE HAD COME to the village back in the forties, one of
that gallant band of midwives who travelled the rough
roads of rural Ireland by bike or pony-and-trap to
deliver babies until the need for their services disappeared.
In 1930 she had gone to Dublin as a young girl to train as a
midwife and on finishing her training had been appointed to
a maternity hospital in Lower Leeson Street. Then she
returned to Cork where she joined the staff of St Kevin's
nursing home, and when a vacancy arose she came back to
Bandon to work in Miss Beamish's Home. In 1943 she was
appointed by the Southern Health Board as local midwife in
Innishannon. Her district covered a wide area and her only
means of transport was a bicycle.

The Nurse was of medium height and her ample figure
exuded serenity; she had a warm and comforting smile and
in later years acquired the air of being everybody's favourite
grandmother. Her long, pale face was framed with soft grey
hair and though her figure had filled out over the years her
hands and feet remained slim and dainty. She never raised
her gentle voice and her small hands were fast and efficient.
You felt in her presence that no matter what emergency
arose she would be in control. During my traumatic days of
early motherhood she called regularly and calmed me with
her reassuring advice. When medical calamity befell any
household in the village we ran to the Nurse's house for help.

During her years as local midwife she brought seven
hundred children into the world and was proud to claim that
she never lost a baby. She always referred to them as her
babies, even after they had had babies of their own. She
spoke with great feeling, too, about the mothers.

"They were great women," she said, "there is no other way to describe them. They were patient, strong, grateful people. No matter how humble the home and how large the family, the new baby was welcomed and there was rejoicing. The father was proud, the other children excited, and the grandparents were happy."

She was the first person that the mother called on to talk about her pregnancy, which they sat down to discuss over a cup of tea. Over the following months they visited each other regularly while the nurse supervised such things as weight, veins and other details. There were no vitamin pills in those days but she sometimes recommended the drinking of stout or a mixture of milk and stout as extra nourishment. Many mothers worked quite hard during pregnancy and often cycled, which kept them very fit.

As soon as the time came for the baby to be born "going for the Nurse" was a job to be entrusted to somebody reliable, usually the father. If he went to collect her in the pony-and-trap then she travelled in comfort, though over the years she experienced all sorts of different means of transport. On one occasion a farm cart with a bag of hay in the middle of it arrived to escort her, on another a horse-and-butt which the farmer had been using during the day to draw cow-dung from his farmyard to the fields, and in his rush for the Nurse had forgotten to wash out. Once a butt arrived that did not need washing as most of the base was missing, and the Nurse was carried along with her legs dangling over the rough, mud-spattering road. Sometimes the messenger arrived on foot and then she pulled out her bike and cycled, often in bad weather, deep into the country.

She came prepared to stay overnight or for as long as she was needed, and brought with her no form of painkiller except her reassuring presence and medical know-how. But although she did not dispense any drugs she still administered therapy and alleviated pain in her own way. She sat with the mother and held her hand, comforting her during her labour. She instructed and encouraged and always she prayed, and as she herself recalled, "The mothers prayed too. We would pray together and it all helped. I trusted in God for everything. I always felt close to God in my work through the years. He always helped me to get to my mothers when they needed me. And," she would add once more, with admiration ringing in her voice, "they were great women."

On many occasions the mother had her own mother present at the birth and often a good neighbour. The Nurse was high in her praise of the neighbours and the support they provided. When asked about the fathers and if any of them were present at the birth, she said, "No, it was unheard of in those days. But they were always near by keeping the fire going to boil water and to make tea, and the children helped him as well so it was a real family affair."

When the baby had been safely delivered the mother had to stay in bed for seven to ten days and the Nurse called every day. Usually the baby was baptised the day after it was born, even though it meant that the mother could not be present; often it was the Nurse or the godmother who took the baby to the church.

Hers were the hands that welcomed many a new life into the world, and they were also the ones that eased many a tired one out of it. When a death was slow and laboured and relatives found it difficult to cope on their own, the Nurse came quietly to the rescue like a serene swan gliding over troubled waters. She sat by the bed soothing the dying and sustaining the living, and when life had finally ebbed away she laid out the dead person with dignity and the minimum of fuss.

Her own life had not been without sorrow: her husband had died suddenly and left her with two small children. Her mother had come to live with her then and she had been able to keep on working, and she was helped too by the generosity of her neighbours, a kindness which she never forgot. "The people of Innishannon were outstanding and it was many a

fine bag of potatoes and vegetables that I got in those days."
When in later years her house was damaged by fire her
neighbours came together again to help her to rebuild it.

A job she adopted as she grew older was decorating the
altar with Nonie and later Ellie, and preparing the crib at
Christmas. She who had brought so many children into the
world enjoyed the annual preparation for the Divine Child.
Every morning she walked up the steep hill to Mass and
when she could no longer walk she was brought by
wheelchair.

As befitted a person who had laid out so many people in
their own homes she, too, died peacefully at home where she
had been cared for by her family. That night as I looked
down at her face, tranquil in death as it had been in life, I
remembered how she had described "her mothers" and
thought, "You were a great woman."

Portrait of a Village

WITH THE GRADUAL departure of the old people from the village, the pattern of coming together casually at the corner and in the houses died out and was replaced by a more structured social system. There was a corresponding increase in the number of organisations, all of which hinged around the parish hall, the Bridge hall and the Rovers' dressing rooms. I was never an organisation person but when an art class started in the Bridge hall I knew that this was something to satisfy the inner me. It was an opportunity that I had always hoped would come my way, because deep within since childhood had lain a slumbering ambition to become an artist. Not a great artist, just one capable of producing a recognisable picture on canvas. There was no passionate dream to walk in the footsteps of Turner, simply a hunger to create.

Our artist teacher who lived outside the village was generous and inspirational. Her motto was: "You can if you think you can." I agreed with her philosophy, but none of my family shared my opinion when they viewed my efforts. My first attempt was to paint a local castle on the banks of the river Bandon, but it came out looking like lumpy porridge. When one of my sons enquired with a puzzled look on his face, "What's that supposed to be?" I knew that I had definitely gone astray. However, I was not daunted. Bitten by the painting bug, I discovered that if an artistic genius had not been sleeping within, a dormant paintaholic had certainly been awakened.

Once a week a small group of us assembled in the hall where we painted, chatted and compared notes on progress. But these weekly sessions were only a small portion of the time I needed to fulfil my increasing hunger to paint. I set myself up in a corner of the kitchen where the smell of paint and turpentine overpowered the normal aromas of baking and cooking. Culinary efforts were far down on my list of priorities. When fellow addicts came into the shop they made their way to the kitchen, where we discussed perspective, depth and different colours. My sons who came looking for late dinners rolled their eyes to heaven and prayed for a return to normality. However, when school lunches were contaminated by turpentine they decided that enough was too much. In the interest of family health I was evicted from the kitchen and ordered upstairs to an old attic where the lighting was better and the climate not so critical.

The threat of strangely flavoured sandwiches had been removed, but a new danger now manifested itself. Once I had escaped to the attic I felt no inclination to come back down. Hungry faces peered around the door, enquiring as to the lack of bubbling saucepans on the downstairs Aga, but they were dismissed imperiously with a sweep of the paintbrush, or threatened with a palette knife and a wail of "Don't break my concentration!" My maternal instinct became buried beneath the profusion of colours running around my brain, and my need to get them co-ordinated and onto canvas. The pictures were in my mind but getting a bridge built from there to the canvas was the problem.

If you enjoy doing something you can only get better at it and gradually the pictures began to take shape. Downstairs in the kitchen I had my own panel of art critics ready to offer opinions when I placed my artistic efforts on top of the fridge for their appraisal. There was one trait that all my children had inherited from my father which I sometimes regretted, and that was his honesty. They were blunt and direct in their criticism and if they judged anything to be "fairly good" I knew that it just had to be brilliant.

Painting opens your eyes to the world around you. You see derelict sites and old stone walls in a new light. Trees in all seasons and the footpaths in the nearby woods in autumn became fascinating to watch. Our painting group exchanged ideas and we never tired of discussing the same topics: a common bond united us. Eventually we decided to go public and hold an exhibition.

This was to be no ordinary exhibition: it was to be a celebration of pictures, flowers and shared enjoyment. We came together one Saturday and scrubbed out the parish hall; everybody brought flowers, driftwood and anything else that they thought would add interest to the exhibition. One of the group who was a member of a flower club created beautiful flower arrangements which filled the hall with their colour and fresh smells. Then we arranged the pictures on the walls. Pictures and flowers blended together in a riot of colour.

Late on Saturday night as we viewed our exhibition we felt a glow of pride. The whole hall was a glorious mix of colour and light. Willing and unwilling husbands had come to assist with the layout. The exhibition was not to be about selling pictures (many of us had very little to sell by the time family members had decorated their walls with our work). It was about sharing our enjoyment, and we hoped that the whole parish would come.

On a beautiful June Sunday a retired English major who lived near the village and had been a well-known watercolour artist in his day opened the exhibition. Due to the noise of passing traffic and the fact that he had a deep, throaty voice which rumbled beneath his red cravat, we did not hear one word he said. But it made no difference to the sense of occasion that prevailed. Locals poured into the hall and were joined by passing tourists. Two of our group sat inside the door welcoming people as they came in and the rest of us drifted around the hall making sure that everybody felt welcome and enjoyed themselves. All day people poured in, and after the cows had been milked the farmers came. Later still, when the pubs had closed, all the happy drinkers came to have a look at what we had on exhibition.

It was a success beyond all our expectations. When they had viewed the work on display some people went home to call out other members of their households because they felt that they were missing something worthwhile. The whole parish came to have a look at the many aspects of the village and scenes from around the parish which we had painted. But an old man captured the spirit of the whole day for me when he stood in front of a picture of an old rusty, broken-down shed which was hanging on the wall and modestly priced at £50.

"By God," he said, "it takes some bating to paint a picture of my own shed, and try to charge me £50 to take it home to look at it."

The Carers

THE WARM JULY sun poured in through the stained glass windows of the little church, casting coloured shadows on the heads of the silent congregation. The sounds of the singing birds came through the open windows. A pigeon cooed peacefully. Into the silence Fr John's soft voice flowed with the wonder and the love of God.

It was a day of rest set aside from the ordinary, a day to meditate, to think and to make space in the mind for things other than the practical. Outside the church the garden was a sea of colour. The flowers like waves of prayer celebrated the beauty of nature and the glory of God. They were nurtured and cared for by Brother Mitchell, and when you saw him kneeling at work in his flower beds, it was to know that prayer took different forms in this holy place.

Early that morning I had walked up the tree-lined avenue while the dew still clung to the surrounding hills. Through the trees in the nearby field I could see horses appear and disappear in the drifting mist. A cock pheasant crowed on the headland, his bright feathers contrasting with the dark green briar-covered ditch. As I stood to listen and to watch, a hare shot past, its speed startling me. The countryside was celebrating the birth of a new day.

St Patrick's Upton, just up the road from our village, is a special place where the people of God not only preach his word but put it into practice daily. Here priests and nuns care for the adult mentally handicapped and give them a useful, dignified lifestyle. People who could not survive in the outside world have a special, caring world created for them here. Yet they are part of our community; every summer the entire parish comes together to run the Upton Steam Rally to raise funds for them. The steam rally was the brainchild of Fr Con and in its early years I catered for the steam-engine men in our guest-house. Because it took off better than anyone had expected we had moments of panic when we had more men than beds, but Fr Con was calm and serene and brought us all smiling through the chaos. He has now gone to heaven but his rally is still oiling the financial wheels of Upton.

On that June day as I walked through Brother Mitchell's flowers I watched the handicapped people sitting on the grass listening to a football match on the radio. Spanning in years from twenty to sixty, they sat together in groups laughing and shouting with excitement at the match. A little apart from the others Ned walked, picking daisies with the joy of childlike discovery in his happy face. A child in the body of an adult, he carried the joys of childhood around in his head. Standing there I felt that I was in the presence of something beyond my understanding. Later that day as we gathered around the altar in a celebration of the love of God I thought of Ned, and later still I wrote this poem.

Battered Chalice
God's day,
The birds and sun
Celebrate his creation.
You pick the daisies
With such joy in your hands;
Little child in the body of a man,
You are the host
In a battered chalice.
"Daoine le Dia,"* old people said,
And how wise they were
Because you live within
The circle of God's arm;
Not for you
The snares of this world,
You walk above man's narrow vision.

*God's people

THE CARERS

That evening as I walked back along the avenue I met Sister Agatha leading a row of "the lads" by the hand. They, too, held hands to help each other along, walking slowly while she patiently answered questions and explained different things to them.

Upton runs on a reservoir of patience. One evening a few years earlier my mother and I had walked through the grounds and met up with Fr Jimmy who, in answer to my mother's questions, had shown her around the whole place. He never mentioned hurry; it seemed as if he had all the time the time in the world. When I had come to Innishannon he had been a clerical student, and over the years I had seen grow in him the serenity of his chosen vocation. His work takes him all over the world but he feels he belongs here in Upton.

I went in through the white iron gate on the left of the avenue to the small graveyard where the Upton priests have been buried down through the years. These priests have not confined their efforts to Upton. They have a Home for the Blind in Dublin and have carried their help to people all over the world. Often where you find the blind and broken you will find religious orders helping them to cope. But though they have worked in many places they have come back here at the end of the day when their life's work is done. This small green corner beneath the trees overlooking the fields of Upton is a peaceful resting place.

Verbal Artist

BLACK NED SWEPT in the door, balancing on the ball of one foot while swinging the other one like the pendulum of a clock. I had not seen him for six months, during which time he had had a hip replacement operation, but his gait was exactly as before. New ball joints or old, Ned's natural rhythm was the same.

During the early days of our guest-house he and other steam-engine men had stayed with us for the Upton Rally. They were a friendly, good-humoured bunch who came together from all corners of Ireland. They drank, laughed and played outrageous pranks on each other throughout the entire weekend. Once when Ned boasted about his sexual prowess one of his friends slapped him on the back and said, "Ned, I'm sure you're a terror in the bed," and ever after that we referred to him as "the terror in the bed."

Now he growled at me in his deep gravely voice: "You're some bitch! Never told me that the Steam Rally was going to be on television." His threw his long arm around me, nearly crushing half a dozen ribs in the process, tore his stubbly jaw across my face like a cheese-grater and planted a moist, porter-flavoured kiss on the top of my nose. "I shouldn't call to see you at all after what you did to me, not saying anything about that programme. You know I'd have enjoyed watching it," he complained.

"Will you quiet down," I protested. "I have it on video so you can watch it in comfort." As I led him along the corridor he chuckled loudly and slapped me across the backside.

"Women," he told me confidently, and I sensed that he was trying to annoy me, "are like horses. You must handle them well and let them know that you like them."

146

"And do horses like a slap across the rump?" I demanded.

"Undoubtedly," he declared. "They are sensitive in that area, and women ..."

"Ned," I intervened before he could develop his point, "sit down there and try to stay quiet while you watch what you are complaining you missed." He threw himself into the chair in front of the television and rubbed his long, brown hands together in anticipation.

As he watched the programme he laughed uproariously when he recognised his friends on screen and slapped his knee with one hand. One of the children brought him a whipped ice-cream from the shop and, looking solemnly at the surprised child, he demanded without a smile on his face, "Any bones in that?" When the programme was over he returned to the supermarket to do some shopping.

Back in the kitchen I put the kettle on the Aga, set the table and picked up a cake from the worktop which I assumed one of the children had brought in for Ned's tea. As we had our tea Ned brought me up to date with all his news. Though he lived a good many miles away I knew some of his neighbours, as they had stayed with us over the years.

"Do you remember Dan Moran?" he demanded, leaning across the table.

"I don't," I said slowly, trying to place the man in question.

"Yerra, you should remember him," Ned insisted forcefully. "A big awkward devil. He is the only fellow you ever saw to come in the door with his arse hitting the two sides of it at the same time. If he sat across the table here from you he'd be the length of it."

"Oh! I remember him." Ned's graphic description had brought him to life.

"Well now," Ned continued, "last week he passed down in front of my place with a tractor and trailer and drove into one of his own fields. The brother-in-law was with him and they spent the whole day erecting two pillars and a gate onto the road. Could you imagine that now? Taking a whole day to

147

do that and the two of them at it? Well, when it was time to go home in the evening the two of them sat up on the tractor and drove out the gap, taking the gate and pillars with them because the trailer was too wide. Could you bate that?"

I looked across at Ned. With his long black hair and sallow skin he had a Spanish look about him, and as he told his story there was no trace of a smile in his sloe-black eyes.

"The same Dan," he continued, "went to the mart a few months ago and bought a pair of boots off the Chape Johns. When he was passing home he called in for the tay and when he was sitting across the table he took off one of the boots and handed it to me. It was eighteen inches long and had a pound of nails in it. 'That's a grand boot,' I told him and he handed me the other one. I declare to God wasn't it six inches shorter and had no toecap like the first one! 'Dan,' I told him, 'they saw you coming. You haven't a pair at all.' 'Well the dirty bastards,' he said, 'I'll tear them asunder,' and he went back to the mart every week for months but the Chape Johns were too smart for him, they never showed up there again."

When Ned stopped to draw breath I asked: "Is Dan married?"

"He's more than married," he assured me, "to a power of a woman. When he got married first he got pneumonia. He was used to sleeping alone, you see, and he caught a chill after the sudden heat. She must be more than sixteen stone. A lot more of a woman than you, now."

Ned could talk for hours. However long he talked I was content to listen, but he had a long road ahead of him so reluctantly he finished his tea. Then he went to gather up his shopping. "Where's my cake?" he said.

"What cake?"

"The bloody cake I bought in your shop to take home to the missus."

"Oh! My God, Ned," I gasped, "we're after eating it."

"Well, Jasus," he said, "'twould take a Cork woman to give me my own cake for my tay!"

"That Could Be Handy Some Day"

IF EVER I decide to sue for divorce I will cite Dev's coat as co-respondent. Clothes, my beloved believes, should not be cast aside but allowed the dignity of dying of old age. He has a pre-marriage overcoat, a pure wool ankle-length model, which would be very suitable to wear if he intended to creep out on dark foggy nights to pounce on innocents from the shadows of alleyways. With no reflection on the nocturnal habits of the man in question, we have christened it Dev's coat. Every few years when I become infected with spring-cleaning fever I bravely bring it out of the wardrobe with a final farewell in mind for it. I hold it up hopefully, but yet again I hear, "There is many a man would be glad of that fine coat." What I am reluctant to tell my nearest and dearest is that that man died about twenty years ago! So back into the wardrobe it goes again.

Teenage sons are like octopuses in that they grow interests in all directions, and attached to each interest comes an extraordinary amount of gear. The football stage brings boots, shin-guards, helmets, footballs and hurleys of all sizes, strengths and suitabilities. Add to that the fact that their father has been chairman, treasurer and secretary of the Valley Rovers and many other clubs, and over the years has brought home all the paraphernalia of high office, some of which remains permanently to choke our drawers and to fall on top of us from high shelves. Glorious years of refereeing gave a statue of Our Lady a referee's whistle dangling on a black shoelace to wear around her neck. Sometimes another one hung off the leg of the bed, which caused me to think that he might penalise me for unfair tackling. Yet whenever a match was to be refereed both whistles disappeared simultaneously. Every drawer in the house was turned upside down, to a background chant of, "Why don't ye let things where I put them? No one could find anything in this bloody house." As I helped search boxes and rummage through cupboards, I eyed Our Lady accusingly, and wondered where she had hid the whistle this time.

The music stage left behind a collection of records and record players, tapes and tape recorders in various stages of disrepair. One son took his love of music a step further, and this resulted in a few stringless guitars propped drunkenly behind the seldom-opened door of a dumping room. If you burst in they fell in front of you and you nearly broke your neck falling over them. Add to this a Rolf Harris play-by-itself gadget, a piano-accordion that was meant to turn an enthusiastic twelve-year-old into a tuneful Dermot O'Brien, and a silent piano standing accusingly in the corner waiting for a renewal of that interest which was once a burning desire to become a concert pianist. Another relic of the music phase were pop magazines fronted by bare-chested guitar players grinning in agony as if suffering was a delightful experience. Every inch of wall-space was covered with wild-looking rock groups.

The call-of-the-great-outdoors period resulted in an assortment of fishing rods draped across one wardrobe, waiting to take the eye out of you, while a shotgun stood menacingly behind the door, inviting me on bad days to put an end to it all. A burst of enthusiasm for model railways ran rings round one bedroom. Tracks were laid along the wall and down a steep hillside between bunk beds to the floor; branch lines, points and signals stretched from window to door. This was the consuming interest of the two older lads and they planned their railways against a very realistic background of mountains and towns. So realistic was it in fact that one night while their two older brothers were out the two younger ones decided to test the ability of the landscape to handle flooding. Unfortunately there was no Ark on hand,

and everything was lost in the deluge. This led to the Thirty Days War in our house, with father on the side of the stronger, older forces and the female protecting her young. So it has been since time began.

Under each bed were boxes of past interest, but the one that had held all minds was the one containing little plastic model soldiers with accompanying artillery. Lego had been used with these to create military layouts that took hours of planning and military manoeuvres. But my young generals, contrary to all army procedures, had often abandoned the battlefield. On many an early morning visit to the bathroom I had squealed in agony on treading barefoot on a Russian soldier poised for action and attacking me from an unfair angle. My hoover had sucked up several lost soldiers who had wandered away from the main force, and had subsequently gone AWOL in the bin. The obsessive interest in war raged for a few years; binders full of *The World at War* and the *Battle of Britain* packed the shelves. Model kits were purchased and replicas of huge British bombers flew across one ceiling. When you entered that room you tended to duck automatically to avoid enemy fire.

Model car fever was an illness to which they all fell victim. In later years this led to the purchase of an old banger; scrap was collected from surrounding dumps and cluttered up the back porch before finally being welded into a model of dubious vintage. This car mania saw stacks of car magazines rise steadily and gather dust under each bed. Posters of model cars vied for attention with pictures of less mechanical but much more curvaceous models. Motor-bike madness soon followed. Black leather boots reminiscent of Hitler's jackboots tripped up unwary people along the corridor; crashhelmets made comfortable beds for stray cats and their padding and straps exercised the jaws of our two badly behaved dogs. Black leather jackets finished off the macho look, which was only finally abandoned when my young man in his flying machine shot over the roof of a hesitant motorist and landed head first in Billy's forge.

On the death of Jacky and Peg we inherited enough religious pictures and statues to furnish an entire monastery with objects of pious zeal. In our irreverent household these objects of religious devotion were elevated to a corner of the attic but they made annual pilgrimages downstairs when the fervour of May altars and Corpus Christi processions hit enthusiastic twelve-year-olds. Such wide-eyed innocence turned to unbelieving cynicism with the sophistication of teenage years. Statues and holy pictures were pushed under beds and hidden at the back of wardrobes to gather dust.

In contrast to all the male military power my daughter's room was a haven of curly-haired dolls and cuddly teddies. Some of the older ones, admittedly, had been loved to exhaustion, but to throw any of them away would have amounted in my girl's eyes to murder. My resolve never failed to weaken when faced by rows of her dilapidated furry friends.

My husband – and the father of the previous offenders – is a man who believes that nothing should be thrown away because "it might come in handy" some day. Maybe that is why I am still around, so perhaps I should be grateful for his philosophy. It has, however, resulted in a build-up of all sorts of outdated objects in our house – and I am not including myself amongst them.

When I go on a spring-cleaning rampage I succeed in disposing of very little of our rubbish, because a wary eye is kept on me until the fever has burned itself out. Then they know that they can all rest easy again amidst their comfortable and familiar clutter. Naturally, when I come to my own room I do not throw away a single item. Everything in there will, I know, definitely come in handy some day!

The Forge

I F YOU DRIVE though our village late on a winter's evening and take the wooded road towards West Cork, a warm glow salutes you through the open door of a small stone building with a roof mellowed by time and weather. Huddled beneath a large beech tree beside the bridge at the entrance to Dromkeen Wood stands Billy's forge, where five generations of his family have shod horses, passing on their trade from father to son down through the years.

Billy began work as a lad of fourteen, learning alongside his two brothers the skills of the blacksmith from their father, Denis, who was known affectionately as "Poundy". It cost five shillings then to shoe a horse, and they turned out eight sets on a good day. They worked on an anvil over 150 years old which Poundy had bought as scrap when the old Bandon railway yard had been closed down in the thirties.

The handling of horses comes naturally to Billy. He has worked with them all his life and treats them as individuals. Their shoes are made in his own forge and once he has fitted a pair he can make them afterwards from memory. From a tall and narrow chimney white smoke drifting up through the trees signals that work is in progress. An infinite variety of iron pieces hang off the stone walls and lie scattered around the floor. Billy wears a brown knitted jumper and comfortable tweed cap, and fastens a leather apron around his front. A small, wiry, agile man, he folds himself over the long legs of frisky horses and soothes them with a special kind of one-to-one communication. Flaring nostrils and quivering ears soon ease into relaxation under Billy's deft touch and steadying words. In this small building horses take precedence over people, and consideration for them and their comfort is the first priority. Over time Billy has built up a wealth of knowledge on horses' ailments, and often he effects a cure when veterinary medicine has failed.

Once hairy-hoofed farm horses clomped in here to have their heavy shoes replaced, but horses were no longer used on the land after the late fifties and early sixties. For a while Billy diversified into welding to fill the gap but gradually riding and racing stables were started up around the county and a different kind of horse found its way in through the forge door. Now horse-boxes from a wide circle of riding and racing stables park outside, and slender-legged and elegant thoroughbreds dance in high spirits on the floor of the forge. But though the type of horse has changed, everything else remains the same. Billy loves his work and finds in it fulfilment: the satisfaction of a job well done he has always held in higher regard than the making of money. He knows his trade as if by instinct, his hands holding the secrets of his craft. When he goes out to assess a job he never uses a measuring tape, but simply runs an experienced eye over the project while his fingers do the measuring. Then, with a few apparently casual belts of the hammer, he moulds red-hot iron into precise, exact shape.

Testimony to Billy's craftsmanship stands all around the countryside – in the gate for the old graveyard which he welded free of charge, or the railing which he designed and made for the stage of our new parish hall. He offers this labour to the community with a heart and a half.

As well as being a place for shoeing horses the forge has always been a focal point in the social life of the parish; people from the surrounding countryside seldom go by without calling in to pass the time of day. When the horse was the backbone of farmwork farmers met here and exchanged news. A wet day especially, when it was considered too miserable to work in the fields, was often set aside for going to the forge to shoe the horses. Then when the horse was replaced by the tractor farmers continued to come here by

night or on bad days. It became a kind of men's club and the
only requirement for membership was to have had a long
association with the place.

Late at night as Billy continues to make shoes in preparation for the following day, they come here, soft-voiced and
easy-going countrymen. They sit around on pieces of iron or
lean against the walls, smoking and discussing horses and
racing, the crops and the weather, the state of things gener-
ally in the farming world. Billy is not one for long-winded
dialogue himself; he is content just to throw in a passing
comment here and there as the conversation flows around
him. If you pass in the gathering darkness it is a pleasant
picture to see through the open doorway the orange outlines
of the men illuminated by the dancing glow of the flames.
But as the years go by the number of friends who visit is
dwindling, as many have passed away.

Anything that stands firm in the changing passage of time
gives a stability and continuity to the flowing tide of life that
surrounds it. So it was not surprising that the forge became a
reference centre for visiting Americans wishing to trace their
ancestral roots. If Billy himself was unable to remember who
their relatives might have been, he would check it out.
Whereas modern heritage centres record facts in computer
memories, Billy searched for family history in local minds
with legendary memories and sometimes they came up with
interesting details not to be found in filing cabinets or data
banks. Strangers looking for directions, too, are told to make
the forge the starting point of their search. It stands like a
lighthouse in the parish, the roads beaming from it into the
heart of the countryside. Billy gives a welcome to all who call
seeking his advice or attention. When he was Taoiseach*
Charles Haughey paid him a visit, accompanied by a clatter
of television cameras; the cameras returned later that year
when Billy shod Carty, the horse Tim Severin used in

*Prime Minister

his journey retracing the path of the Crusades. Billy took all the publicity in his stride, regarding it as something not to be taken too seriously.

Only when the big race meetings are on is the forge door closed, for horses have always been both the work and pastime of this family. Billy's brother Paddy was a blacksmith in the Curragh and on retirement became our school bus-driver. He was the ideal man for the job. Patient and understanding from long years of handling horses, the children loved him. He became the bosom pal of my young daughter. One evening during her first year at school she was walking down the hill when a few of the older boys started to jostle each other below her. Afraid to pass by them she started to cry. Paddy, driving past in the bus, saw her problem and stopped to pick her up. It was the start of a firm friendship. When he died she got a mortuary card which had a photograph of Paddy on it, and it took pride of place on her bedroom wall between rows of pony posters. Paddy is in familiar company.

Down through the years village children have gone to Billy with small wheelbarrows and broken bikes, and he welds them back together again. Older children waiting for the bus take shelter in the forge, and if they come late Billy flags down a reliable motorist to see that they get to school. When my young daughter and her friends used go to Dromkeen Wood on picnics I would tell them to tell Billy where they were, because I knew he would keep an eye on them.

The horse is so much a part of Irish life that there will always be a need for shoeing facilities, but a forge such as Billy's will not provide it. He is the last in a long line of blacksmiths, and his way of doing things will go with him. The glow from the fire of his forge is the last flicker in a way of life that is almost gone.

My Place

WHEN I OPEN my eyes in the morning I can see through the bedside window, without having to lift my head off the pillow, the old tower at the end of the village. Some mornings it stands cold and grey against the dark woods, a sentinel on guard over the river. On other mornings it is a milky white ghost appearing and disappearing in the swirling river-mists, while the woods in the background are a soft shroud around its shoulders. But on summer mornings it salutes the dawn upright and arrogant, crows flying above its turrets, their demon blackness contrasting with the pale pinks of the morning sky. On such a morning, when the dawn curtains are drawn back on a glorious new day, I feel like dancing out of the house and into the woods.

When I go down the stone steps into Shippool Wood I leave above and behind me the everyday world. It is almost like going down into a rabbit burrow; down there, under the quiet arms of the trees, I can walk in a pool of peace. The trees are set on a sloping hillside with the river washing their toes, and as I walk along the winding path the river glints occasionally through the dense greenery. Sometimes the sun filters down from above and the riverlight and sunlight fill the dark green wood with dancing patches of light and shade.

Walking through the moist green semi-darkness I see ahead a bright inpouring of light at a clearing. There I can sit and watch the swans on the river. A river surrounded by woods is twice blessed, as the beauty on its banks is mirrored in its depths. The large white swans drift effortlessly along and as I resume my own journey I find paths cushioned by pine needles and years of fallen leaves. Mossy banks along

157

the way offer comfortable seats. Feathery heather and droop-
ing moist ferns kiss my ankles, and occasionally an over-
hanging branch touches my cheek with its soft green leaves.

In the wood Mother Nature wraps her arms around you
and makes you feel cherished and at home. Overhead the
leaves sigh a welcome and beneath them an endless variety
of tree-trunks salute you on your way: the young trees with
their smooth expressionless faces, the more mature ones
curved and furrowed, and the ancient tree-trunks with
masses of delved hollows and humps recording the passage of
decades. To rub your fingers over their mossy lichen cover is
to feel at one with the passage of time in this peaceful wood.

Here I can listen to a thousand rustling whispers in the
undergrowth, but as I walk from deep green shadows into
splashes of light I am aware that the river is my silent companion along the way. Where the path climbs steeply upwards tree
roots protruding from the ground act as steps, and where the
path slopes downwards their trunks are supporting handrails.

At the bottom of the incline the path runs along the river-
bank and here you can sit and look across to the little quayside village of Kilmacsimon. The village and the small boats
tied up along the quay are reflected in the deep water. This is
the centre-point of a walk through Shippool Wood; I could sit
here for hours listening to the tidal water lapping against the
bank as it changes direction. Late in the evening the sunset
can be seen through the branches of an old tree that clings to
the river-bank by its roots, its long arms stretched out above
the water and reflected in its depths. Then the crows return
like black messengers across the sky to the wood on the other
side, and once they arrive they fill the air with their chatter
like old friends exchanging gossip after a day out.

While this wood in summer is a green wonderland, in
autumn it takes on a russet glow. To walk through Shippool
Wood then is to have a golden carpet spread beneath your feet.
All around is the rustle of falling leaves, breathing their last
as they glide earthward. A soft breeze sends the branches

creaking and more leaves drift down. This is the world of the autumn wood. At Christmas time the holly trees celebrate the festive season with trailing dark-green branches of red berries.

Leaving the riverside the climb is steep, but the roots of the trees criss-crossing the way provide a firm foothold. This path leads back to the road high above the Bandon river and Shippool Castle. Up along the wooded valley the village of Innishannon lies in the distance. The road to the right here leads to Kinsale; on the way at a turn you can stand on the ditch and look down over the river broadening out as it heads for the harbour, and see the wide countryside spread out before you like a patchwork quilt.

But the road to the left leads home to Innishannon. Past Shippool Castle the river accompanies you along the way, until you part with it at the "Found Out". In earlier days this was a shebeen where late night drinkers and smugglers cele-brated, and sometimes they were "found out" on the premises by raiding constabulary. When you come to the hill leading down into the village you are standing at the top of The Rock. Below you Innishannon lies between the trees.

Shippool is the wood for summer and autumn, but Drom-keen Wood, which looks over the village from the hill across the river, is the winter and spring-time wood. During the bleak winter months trees sleep beneath a dull blanket of grey and brown, their trunks reaching down into the cold black river in the valley below. They wear tattered coats before the sharp winter winds whip them naked. Their stark beauty revealed, they stretch their gaunt limbs heavenward like crucifixion figures. On hard frosty nights you can see from the village the trees on the hilltop standing with their black arms outlined against the cold blue sky, like figures waiting for the resurrection of spring.

With the coming of spring a tinge of green can be seen in the evening light, and after a few weeks the bluebells carpet the hill. Beside the high pathway they run in waves of billowing blue as far as the eye can see. From here you can look down over the village and in a special little corner see the river disappear beyond the bridge into another wood in the distance. By late September that same view has turned into an interwoven tapestry of scarlet, browns and yellows.

In Innishannon we are surrounded by woods on both sides of the river and to drive along the road in the autumn from Bandon to Innishannon and on to Kinsale must surely be one of the most glorious journeys in the country. The long expanse of wood stretches before you, and when you think that there can be nothing more beautiful than the trees at Dundaniel Castle you come to the view at Innishannon Bridge, then to Shippool Castle, and on to Kinsale. The trees are multi-coloured, a glorious profusion of golden browns. They create a soft, voluptuous panorama and give the illusion that one could sink into their softness.

Sometimes I like to leave the village behind and walk up along the quiet roads around Upton, especially on a warm evening when the ditches are draped with summer flowers and yellow woodbine intoxicates your senses with its wild smell. As I walk by the scented ditches I can listen to the cows chewing tufts of grass or stand at rusty gates along the way and watch noble horses graze together or canter in high spirits around the field. Passing through the grounds of St Patrick's, flowers lie like a rosary around the monastery, and I can call in to the little chapel for a soothing prayer.

Coming down the road from Upton back into the village the tall, elegant steeple of our hillside church salutes one through the trees. On a moonlit night the stars cluster above its dark bulk and the moon sometimes rests on its back, sheltering in the angle between the ridged roof and steeple.

I fell in love with Innishannon the first time I saw it, and my life here has been a continuing love affair with this very special village, which I now think of as my place.